History of the Church in Peru

Written by

Ancient & Modern-day Prophets & Apostles,
General Authorities & Mission Presidents,
Missionaries & Members

of

The Church of Jesus Christ of Latter-day Saints

Compiled by

Dale Christensen

ISBN #978-1517333430

© by DaleChristensen1995

Dedication

This book is dedicated to my son Samuel whose ancestors came to this Promised Land with Father Lehi. They walked the ancient Americas and built the mighty Incan Empire. In his veins flows the blood of a chosen nation and in his heart is the anticipation of the promised blessings of the Lord. I love Samuel. I love the Peruvian people and those who ministered among them. I love Peru. This is my gift to all of you.

Acknowledgments

Thanks to Karen Lais and Coni Roller who masterfully and speedily typed the highlighted passages and text into the computer. The manuscript will be sent to past Mission Presidents who served in Peru for their additional suggestions and input. It is my desire to see this book be printed in both English and Spanish (English on the left page and Spanish on the right). In this format the readers may read in either language and improve their skills in the other language as they do so. To my dear wife, Mary-Jo, who served faithfully as my missionary companion and to my children, Teresa Joy, Samuel, Jonathan and Tamara, and all the missionaries who have served in Peru, I pay tribute and express my love and gratitude for their great contributions and dedication.

"These were days never to be forgotten . . ."
Oliver Cowdry

Prelude

The first thoughts of preparing a history of the church in Peru came to me shortly after receiving instructions that the Peru Lima South Mission home was to become the Missionary Training Center for the northern part of South America. In preparation to move the mission home, the missionaries and I began the long task of cleaning out every cupboard and closet containing dozens of boxes full of all the papers and records from the beginning of the Andes Mission. This mission home had been the first property purchased by the church in this part of South America and it still contained many historical records and artifacts that had not been taken when the Area Administration Office had been opened.

The first sorting produced many original legal documents and baptismal records that the Area Administration Office was very grateful to receive. All the mission histories and many statistics were carefully saved in one large box and the rest was discarded. Several missionary couples, some who were soon ending their missions, kindly agreed to help organize and type the material to be preserved in a history volume. They worked long and hard to help condense these volumes of information into one stack of paper about three inches high. This stack was carefully put into a box along with other items and there it stayed until we finished our mission.

This box was shipped home with our few belongings and was soon stored along with other boxes of books in my brother's basement until we became settled. Almost seven years passed before I finally opened that particular box on a Saturday afternoon just a few weeks ago. I began to read through these several hundreds of pages, and immediately I again felt an overwhelming urge to complete this work in its first edition form so it could be put into the hands of the Peruvian people.

As I edited and selected passages from the material that had been prepared years earlier, I became concerned about who this history should be written for and what criticism it might receive from the skeptics. The thought came to my mind that perhaps these were some of the thoughts Mormon had struggled with as he prepared the Golden Plates. No doubt he had many manuscripts and sets of metal plates to review and select from.

It is impossible to imagine this book having even a small portion of the impact on readers that the Book of Mormon has had. But, this I will say, that I have felt tremendous appreciation and gratitude for those who pioneered the Lord's work in Peru. I also feel an overwhelming spirit of love for all the missionaries, Mission Presidents, church leaders and members and for the multitudes who may read this history. Perhaps it may be something special for them to take into the millennium.

Table of Contents

Title Page	1
Dedication & Acknowledgments .	2
Prelude	3
Table of Contents . . .	5
Introduction	6
Chapter 1 - Dawning Of A New Day	12
Chapter 2 - The South American Mission	17
Chapter 3 - Missionary Moments .	33
Chapter 4 - An Acorn To An Oak .	44
Chapter 5 - The Andes Mission .	54
Chapter 6 - Making Progress . .	66
Chapter 7 - Making History . .	82
Chapter 8 - Hope Through Adversity	88
Chapter 9 - Earthquake . .	116
Chapter 10 - The Rosebud Begins To Blossom	144
Chapter 11 - A Time of Re-dedication	154
Chapter 12 - Recent History . .	169
Chapter 13 - DEDICATION: Lima Peru Temple	192
Chapter 14 - The Stone Rolls Forth .	210

INTRODUCTION

Cuzco Yacta is the Qechua name for the magnificent city of Cuzco located high in the altiplano among the Andes mountains of Peru. Literally translated, this name means "the umbilical cord of the world" or "where all life began." Ancient Indian legends describe the creation, the flood, and a visit by the white-bearded God named "Viracocha." Peru was the birthplace of ancient civilizations and is a sacred part of this Promised Land.

In the beginning, when the world was created, but before the land was divided, "God planted a garden eastward in Eden, and there He put the man and woman whom He had formed." (Genesis 2:8) Adam and Eve lived in the Garden of Eden until they were cast out into the lone and dreary world because they had partaken of the fruit of the tree of knowledge of good and evil of which they had been commanded not to partake. Adam tilled the ground, and they began to multiply and replenish the earth as Eve bore children. The everlasting Gospel was preached unto them, and they received the sacred ordinances by the power of God. Adam offered sacrifices in the similitude of the Only Begotten of the Father who is full of grace and truth. Their posterity had free agency to choose between good and evil. Some chose to obey God and others became wicked and followed Satan.

Although there is not much detailed information as to the travels or experiences of Adam's life; we do know that he lived to be 930 years of age. His travels could have been extensive. "Three years previous to the death of Adam, he called" together "the residue of his posterity who were righteous, into the valley of Adam-Ondi-Ahman and bestowed upon them his last blessing." (D&C 107:53) The Prophet Joseph Smith was told on May 19, 1838 that it was here (Spring Hill, Daviess County, Missouri) that "Adam shall come to visit his people" in the last days. (D&C 116:1)

Centuries passed and "God saw that the wickedness of man was great in the earth . . . but Noah found grace in the eyes of the Lord." (Genesis 6:5,7) He built an ark of gopher wood, and he took his family into the ark along with animals of every kind; male and female. Noah, his wife and his three sons and their wives were the only people on the whole face of the earth who survived the great flood which covered the earth after it had rained for forty days and forty nights. The ark rested on another part of the land and later the land was divided. God set a rainbow in the cloud as a token of his covenant that there should not "anymore be a flood to destroy the earth." (Genesis 8:11)

Because of unbelief and wickedness, a great tower was built to reach up to the heavens and to avoid another flood. God was not pleased so he confounded the peoples' languages, and they were "scattered abroad upon the face of all the earth." (Genesis 11:9) Holy men were called of God to preach the Gospel of Jesus Christ to all mankind. Abraham was called and ordained and also tested of the Lord when he was asked to sacrifice his son, Isaac. Isaac's son Jacob, later called Israel, had twelve sons who were the fathers of the twelve tribes of Israel. His son, Joseph, had two sons, Ephraim and Manasseh. Jacob's firstborn son, Reuben, sinned and lost his birthright. It was given to the sons of Joseph. (1 Chronicles 5:1-2) Opportunity to survive the famine later turned to slavery, in Egypt for the children of Israel, but they were led out of captivity by the Prophet Moses. The land of promise was given to the children of Israel and they prospered. Centuries came and went, but those favored by the Lord again fell into darkness. The holy city of Jerusalem was doomed to fall into the hands of the Babylonians.

Approximately 600 years before the birth of the Lord Jesus Christ, during the reign of King Zedekiah, one of the holy prophets named Lehi was commanded by God to leave Jerusalem and, with his family, travel to a promised land. Together with Ishmael and his family, they traveled through the desert until they came to an ocean. There they constructed a large ship and sailed across the ocean to this American continent. This history, as recorded in The Book of Mormon, further tells of a division among these people and the many battles that followed. A great civilization was developed and other more ancient civilizations were discovered. One had originated from a migration at the time of the building of the great tower of Babel when the languages were confounded approximately 2200 years before Christ. (Book of Ether)

The most important and beautiful account in the Book of Mormon is about the visit of Jesus Christ to the ancient Americas after His death and resurrection. At the time of His crucifixion, there were great earthquakes, tornadoes, fire and destruction. The land was raised up by the formation of high mountains while other land sunk into the sea. Then, there followed three days of darkness after which the Savior descended out of heaven and appeared to the people of this land. He showed the people the wounds in His hands and His feet and in His side. He taught these people His Gospel. He organized His church among them, and He promised them that He would come again some day.

For 200 years these people lived in peace and righteousness However, after two centuries they gradually became wicked once again. There was again a great division between the white race and a darker skinned people who are the ancestors of the Peruvian Indians. Because of their wickedness, the white race was completely destroyed, leaving only the darker skinned people. This group of people continued to live in this land until the Conquistadors came to conquer them and rob them of their lands and wealth. The Spaniards also tried to destroy the Inca's religion and ancient beliefs and replace it with Christianity. These descendents of Lehi lived in slavery for centuries until the light of the restored Gospel began to dawn upon the nations of the earth.

Secular history teaches that one thousand years before the Christian Era, the Chavin culture, which is considered the first culture to develop here, flourished. Their history of Peru can be divided into several eras: Pre-Inca, Inca, Discovery and Conquest, Virreynato, Emancipation, Republic. The Incan empire was a great civilization. They held the tradition of the Great White God. Their rulers were four brothers who built temples and great cities. Another legend held by the Incas was that of a liquid that could turn rock to dirt and dirt to rock. The White God was to have walked on water and performed other miracles etc. This people was a tall and well nourished people.

Simultaneously with the liberation of the Spanish rule and monarchy in Peru, God revealed Himself once again to mankind. It was then that the history of The Church of Jesus Christ of Latter-day Saints began, including the history of the church in Peru.

In 1820 Joseph Smith, the boy prophet, was visited by God the Father and His Son Jesus Christ in a grove of trees in the state of New York. The Church of Jesus Christ, the fullness of the Gospel, the priesthood authority and all the saving ordinances were restored through subsequent revelations and visitations by heavenly messengers. The Church of Jesus Christ of Latter-day Saints was organized on April 6, 1830. A detailed history of the Church was kept by Joseph Smith and others. The following pages contain the history of the church as it came to South America, and finally to Peru, and the growth and development of the Kingdom of God in this sacred part of this great Promised Land.

The history of the church in Peru really begins with the visit of Parley P. Pratt to South America in 1851 and 1852. He didn't actually go to Peru or teach any Peruvians, but he focused his prophetic attention on that land, looked upon it from the sea and from its neighbor, Chile, and, in his mind, pondered the way in which the church would someday spring up there. He wished it could have happened in his day, but he saw how it would happen in ours.

Of course, the Lord had done so much in preparation. Nearly a millennium before (II Nephi 5:14-17), Inca legend tells of Manco Capac and Mama Ocllo who had come, like Nephi, to teach the people not war, but husbandry, defense, and a special selflessness that, to this day, characterizes their offspring. Before that, centuries before, the last symbols were etched upon the golden plates of the Book of Mormon and buried, along with all the promises that it contained.

Peru is a beautiful country with a variety of people, cultures and climates. There are the very rich and the very poor who are searching and working for a better life. Lima is a large metropolitan city with many millions of inhabitants, but most of Peru's population live in smaller cities and villages with many families still living in adobe houses and farming by hand or with oxen just as their ancestors have done for centuries.

The west coast of Peru is a desert about 20 miles wide and stretches north to Ecuador and south to the border of Chile. The western slopes of the Andes Mountains are dry and rugged. They look very much like Ben Lomand Mountain in North Ogden, Utah as they rise from sea level to over 16, 000 feet through the Ticlio Pass, the highest railroad pass in the world. The Andes Mountains get their name from the "Andeas" or terraces built by the ancient Incas for agricultural purposes.

The high mountain plains are called the "Alti-plano" and look as if the whole area had been lifted up at the time of Christ's crucifixion. The eastern slopes of the Andes are covered with vegetation and waterfalls cascading off the tops of high mountains. It is called the "dry jungle". The best way to describe this beautiful land is to say that it looks very much like Arnold Friberg's painting that we find in the Book of Mormon of Alma baptizing in the Waters of Mormon. The eastern portion of Peru which borders Brazil is in the flat rain forest jungle where the headwaters of the Amazon River originate.

Doct. & Covts. 49:24 predicts that "the Lamanites will blossom as a rose". This prophecy is literally being fulfilled, and I am so grateful to have been a part of seeing it come to pass. President Spencer W. Kimball told us that we must harvest while the "tide is in" and while the spirit is moving over this people. The same kind of thing that happened in England and Scandinavia during the early days of the Church is now happening in Peru and throughout Latin America. This is their day!

Chapter 1

Dawning of a New Day

In 1851, Elder Parley P. Pratt was called and set apart by the Prophet to take charge of a General Mission to the Pacific, which included California, Hawaii, Australia, Chile, and, of course, Peru. (Autobiography of Parley P. Pratt, p. 370.) "On November 8, 1851, Elder Parley P. Pratt and his wife (Phebe Soper), with Elder Rufus C. Allen, disembarked from the ship *Henry Kelsey* at Valparaiso, Chile. Here they rented a house and commenced to study the Spanish Language. (Encyclopedia History of the Church, by Andrew Jenson, page 810)

These were the first Latter-day Saint missionaries called to South America, having been sent to open the door for the preaching of the restored Gospel of Jesus Christ in that land. The missionaries lived for several months in Valparaiso and for about one month forty miles inland. Unfortunately revolution, civil war and the language difficulties prevented them from accomplishing much and they returned to the United States in May, 1852. For seventy years no further missionary attempts were made in that land. (Melvin J. Ballard: Crusader for Righteousness. Salt Lake City, Chapter 6, p. 75-84, Bookcraft, 1966.)

Thirty years earlier, Jose de San Martin, the Saint with a Sword, had landed near Pisco. It was September, 1820, only a few months after the restoration had begun in the northern hemisphere. It was, in San Martin's analysis: "The greatest day of our revolution." (Historia del Peru by Gustavo Pons Muzzo, p. 121)

From his special vantage point, Elder Pratt took note of this liberation and wrote to his brethren: "Should Peru sustain her liberties, a field is opened in the heart of Spanish America, and in the largest, best informed and most influential city and nation of South America, for the Bible, the Book of Mormon, and the fullness of the Gospel to be introduced." (Autobiography of Parley P. Pratt, p. 400) He noted that "Four-fifths, or perhaps nine-tenths, of the vast population of Peru /is/ of the blood of Lehi," which, in 1852, was a much smaller number, if not percentage, than exists today. "More Indians live in Peru than in any other country in the western hemisphere," writes William Mangin, contributor to the 1984 World Book Encyclopedia.

Elder Pratt had it in his heart to translate the Book of Mormon into Spanish. He felt that, with it, the keys could be turned to the nations entrusted to his care. A living priesthood would be accompanied by "those writings which have the promises of God, the prayers and faith of the ancients, and the power and spirit of Good to work with them in restoring the house of Israel." (Autobiography, p. 401) He also foresaw the need for the missionary force of Peruvian nationals which is now advancing that work: ". . . A door is opening more wide than can be filled very soon in the Spanish language, unless God shall raise up . . . thousands of native teachers . . ." (Autobiography, p. 400)

From Chile, he followed events inside Peru and "had much desire to go to Peru." However, unable to do so, he contented himself to labor to prepare the way for those who would "in due time, be sent . . .in power; knowing that God, who has said certain things, will cause those things to be performed . . ." (Autobiography, p. 401) Elder Pratt's mission came to a close. In the succeeding decades of that century and for the first two of the next, though the vision of the work did not dim, the urgency was replaced by other pressing matters. The preparations of the Lord, however, marched forward in ever wider scope and certainty.

The next step was taken in 1925. In that year, President Heber J. Grant announced a mission to South America and the calling of Elder Melvin J. Ballard to open it. "This assignment was the second great shock of my life," wrote Elder Ballard. (Sermons and Missionary Service of Melvin J. Ballard by Bryant S. Hinckley, p. 90) We recognize how fully and marvelously he carried out this assignment as he was accompanied by Elders Rulon S. Wells and Rey L. Pratt of the First Council of the Seventy.

They traveled from New York to Buenos Aires where, after dedicating the continent, Elder Ballard prophesied: "The work of the Lord will grow slowly for a time here just as an oak grows slowly from an acorn . . . But thousands will join the church here. It will be divided into more than one mission and will be one of the strongest in the church . . . The day will come when the Lamanites in this land will be given a chance. The South American Mission will be a power in the church." It is noteworthy that these words, which would have otherwise been lost to our memory, were thoughtfully recorded for those who would follow. They were recorded by James Vernon Sharp, a young elder who had been serving under President Pratt in the Mexico Mission and had been transferred to South America to carry on the work which Elders Ballard, Wells, and Pratt initiated.

Those beginnings in Argentina have blessed Peru. Many of the early missionaries and converts from Argentina have played important roles. The fast friendship that has existed between those countries since the days of San Martin has been paralleled in the church. This early work in Argentina has been well documented. Less well known, however, is Elder Ballard's and Elder Pratt's 1926 journey of weeks across northern Argentina and up and across the highlands of Bolivia to La Paz. In Bolivia they marveled at the ancient ruins and at the almost undreamed of potential for the work among the children of Lehi. They crossed the international border on Lake Titicaca to Juliaca, Peru. By train, they traveled to

Sicuani and Cuzco, back to Juliaca, to Arequipa, and eventually to Mollendo ("a little place, but beautifully situated on a bluff above the sea," wrote Elder Pratt). From Mollendo they secured passage to New York on the S.S. Essequibo and set sail for home.

The ship stopped one evening in Pisco and loaded cotton. The brethren did not go ashore. But the next morning they awoke to find themselves in the port of Callao. They arose, "went ashore and on up to Lima, the capital of Peru . . . a very old city (of) 230,000 people." (Elder Pratt's Diary) From Lima, they continued north, stopping at the little ports of "Sallaverra" and "Paita" (spellings from Elder Pratt's Diary) before leaving the coastal waters of Peru and sailing through the Panama Canal to North America.

Undoubtedly, time and again these fearless men preached the Gospel of the restoration along their way. Elder Pratt was fluent in Spanish and Elder Ballard was willing to bear testimony at all times and in all places. We know significant efforts were made to proselyte in La Paz both by these leaders and by Elder Sharp, who followed them one year later. But where, within the bounds of modern day Peru, they may have preached the Gospel first is not recorded. Perhaps it was in Juliaca. Perhaps in Cuzco or Arequipa. We do not know. But there is a story about Mollendo which might have been the first missionary story of Peru.

While Elder Sharp was still in Argentina in 1927, he received a message from Elders Ballard and Pratt to travel to northern Argentina and Bolivia. Elder Ballard wanted the missionaries "to see the Indians," as Elder Sharp put it. With his companions, Elder Sharp traveled to Jujuy, the home of San Martin, left them there and proceeded north over the Andes to La Paz, where he labored by himself until his missionary tracts and literature was gone. "What now? he asked himself. But just then a telegram arrived with his release. He crossed Lake Titicaca in a snowstorm. The next morning he was in Peru. It was June 5, 1927. He went to Cuzco and, from there, to Ollantaytambo, the end of the road. Hyrum Bingham was still working on Machu Picchu, but Elder Sharp did not visit him. An impassable terrain and, in Elder Sharp's word, "snakes," kept him from going further. He returned to Juliaca, then took passage for Mollendo via Arequipa.

While still in Argentina and Bolivia, Elder Sharp had received correspondence from Elders Ballard and Pratt asking that he look up the Protestant church in Mollendo. He still remembers that, when he did so, the man who answered said, "Are you the missionary that was promised?" He was reading the Book of Mormon and "A Voice of Warning" that the brethren had left a year earlier. In Elder Sharp's words, "Brother Ballard and Brother Pratt had really made an impression." That promise, made by an apostle, stayed with Elder Sharp. In 1959, he returned as the first Mission President in Peru and sent full-time missionaries to Mollendo.

Once the work began, many general authorities and future presidents of the church visited the saints and missionaries. None is more remembered than Elder Spencer W. Kimball's week-long visit in June, 1964. He was consumingly interested in every place, everything, and every person. Those who tried to maintain his pace were exhausted. To Elder A. Theodore Tuttle's concern that he might wear himself out, he replied: "You do not understand. My life is not in my hands but in the Lord's." Above all else, he wanted to see the people -- not just those that were then members of the church, but the multitudes. They did not recognize him, but he recognized them. That was his second of many visits.

Elders Pratt and Ballard and all those that have followed understood that the promises of the Book of Mormon are and will be fulfilled in the people and land of Peru and in other countries similarly situated.

Chapter 2

The South American Mission

On Thursday, September 3rd, 1925 at a regular council meeting of the First Presidency and Twelve, in the Temple at Salt Lake City, Utah, President Grant announced that the Presidency had been considering for more than a year and a half the question of opening a mission in South America, and they had now concluded that the time had come to do this, and that one of the Twelve should go to head the mission, and that Elder Melvin J. Ballard of the Council of Twelve had been chosen, to have President Rulon S. Wells of the First Council of Seventy, and President Rey L. Pratt of the First Council of Seventy and President of the Mexican Mission, to be his companions: Brother Wells speaking German and Brother Pratt Spanish. This action was unanimously approved by the council.

On September the 4th, the Presidency gave Elder Ballard some instructions concerning the opening of the South American Mission, and advised that the headquarters of the Mission be established in Buenos Aires, Argentina. Correspondence received earlier from Wilhelm Friederichs and Emil Hoppe, converts from Germany then residing in Buenos Aires, had urged that missionaries be sent and reported that some Germans there were awaiting baptism.

After a farewell party for the South American Missionaries, they blessed and set apart for their missions. They left Salt Lake City at 5:15 p.m. November the 3rd, 1925 and traveled over the Union Pacific Railroad to Denver and on to Kansas City, Missouri to Chicago and then onto New York City, arriving on November 10th. Elders Pratt and Ballard with the assistance of the missionaries then purchased a moving picture machine, and a projector for still pictures, to be used in the new Mission.

Leaving New Jersey at 4:00 p.m. November 14, 1925, the Brethren sailed from the Hoboken Pier number 14 on the British S.S. "Voltaire". About sixty missionaries with Sister Roberts were present and sang several of our hymns as the Brethren sailed away. Elder Ballard carried with him credentials and letters of introduction from the mayor of Salt Lake City, the president of the University of Utah, the governor of the State of Utah, and United States senators and ambassadors, all commending him to the confidence and esteem of those to whom he present them.

Typically, Elder Ballard recorded the distance the ship traveled each day and made it a practice to walk five miles or more daily. Eleven laps around the deck made a mile; so he would make this round from fifty to sixty times each day. In this way he kept his weight down and built up his vitality. The sea voyage was a boon to his health. He was free from sickness and enjoyed every day of the journey. There was no waste of time or mental lethargy during the voyage, for every spare moment he studied the Spanish language or read the Book of Mormon in Spanish. He also read the history of South America to acquaint himself with the colonization and pioneering of that land.

On November 29th the boat reached Rio de Janeiro that night at 10:30 p.m. The next two days were spent on shore by the Brethren visiting the beautiful city and its harbor. This was the first time they had set foot on South American soil. When December 5 came, the boat docked at Montevideo, spending most of the day there, while the Brethren visited this unusual city. The boat left that same evening at 4:30 p.m. up the La Plata River for Buenos Aires.

Three weeks after their departure from New Jersey, on December 6, 1925, the boat docked at the harbor of Buenos

Aires, North Basin, at 7:00 a.m. after a voyage of over seven thousand miles, according to the ship's log, in most pleasant weather without a moment's sea sickness for any of the Brethren. They were met at the dock by Brothers Wilhelm Frederichs, Emil Hoppe, their wives, and several friends they had interested in the Gospel.

The Brethren took quarters at the Grand Hotel the first night. At 4:00 p.m. the next day they attended a cottage meeting at the home of Ernst Biebersdorf, Calle Iraia number 1830 Dock Sud., Buenos Aires, Argentina. This being the first meeting held by the Brethren in South America. Besides the Missionaries, there were present nine adults and four children. Four of the adults, Brothers Friederichs and Hoppe and their wives, were members of the Church in Germany. The balance were friends whom they had interested in the Gospel. The services were conducted in the German language. All those present were German people and each of the Brethren spoke; Brother Wells acting as translator.

For the past two years since the arrival of Brothers Friederichs and Hoppe in this country, they had been conducting cottage meetings regularly; Brother Friederichs leading out in this matter, and they had interested a number of people, some of whom were ready for baptism. Some of the seeds that had been planted were now growing, but the harvest was still to be realized.

Soon after arriving, Elder Wells had the first of several severe dizzy spells with excessive vomiting which lasted for several hours. The Brethren moved to Cervantes Hotel, 1367 Rivadavia Street, on account of the excessive charge at the Grand Hotel; ($32.00 pesos) for one room for the three Brethren. At 7:00 p.m., December 10th, another cottage meeting was held at the home of Emil Hoppe. Each of the Brethren spoke on baptism and asked how many understood the first principles of the Gospel, and were willing to join the Church and keep the commandments of the Lord. There were five adults who signified their willingness to do this, and an appointment to baptize them was made. The harvest would soon begin.

The Brethren moved to Santa Fe, No. 1301, Departmento C., to provide better accommodations for Brother Wells. Their quarters consisted of two bedrooms, a study room and a bathroom. The next day, Saturday December 12th, at 7:00 p.m., the Brethren with the saints and those that applied for baptism assembled on the shore of the Rio de La Plata, immediately east of the German electric plant, in Dock Sud. After prayer by Elder Rulon S. Wells, Elder Melvin J. Ballard baptized the following persons in the order named: Anna Kullick, Ernest Biebersdorf, Jacob Kullick, Maria Biebersdorf, Herta Kullick, Elisa Plassmann. These were the first baptisms performed in this dispensation in South America. They were confirmed members of the Church. On Sunday at 4:00 p.m., in the house of Jacob Kullick, at Lanus, the first Sacrament and Confirmation meeting was held.

The following ordinations also took place: Wilhelm Friederichs, to office of Priest by Melvin J. Ballard; Emil Hoppe, to office of Priest by Rulon S. Wells; Ernst Biebersdorf to office of Deacon by Rey L. Pratt; Jacob Kullick to office Deacon by Melvin J. Ballard. And the following children were blessed: Magdalena Friederichs by Rulon S. Wells; Hildegard Hoppe by Melvin J. Ballard; Edith Elizabeth Biebersdorf by Rey L. Pratt; Meta Maria Biebersdorf by Rulon S. Wells. The Sacrament was administered by Elders Rulon S. Wells and Rey L. Pratt, in all this work English, Spanish and German were used. All present bore testimony, except Sister Biebersdorf, and a glorious spirit was manifest.

On the next day they made arrangements to get Bibles from the American and English Bible Societies. They then visited the 3 de Febrero Park, and found a suitable place to offer the dedicatory prayer. The American Ambassador, Mr. P.A. Jay, received them, but was full of his New England prejudices against the Mormons. However, he gave them a letter to Dr. Carlos M. Noel, the mayor of the City of Buenos Aires, who received them graciously and assured them that we had the fullest liberty to establish our mission, and that there would be no hindrance on the part of the government. The mayor was impressed with Elder Pratt's excellent Spanish. Immediately thereafter, a letter was written to President Grant asking that missionaries be sent to South America.

Christmas was the chosen day. On Friday, December 25, 1925, the Brethren left their quarters at 6:00 a.m. and arrived at the place they had previously selected, a natural grove of weeping willow trees, near the bank of the river, in the Park 3 de Febrero. At 7:00 a.m. they sang "The Morning Breaks", "Hail to the Brightness of Zion's Glad Morning" and "An Angel from on High". Elder Rey L. Pratt read from the Book of Mormon, First Nephi 13; 2 Nephi 31, and 3 Nephi 21. Elder Rulon S. Wells read Genesis 29, 22 to 26, after which Elder Melvin J. Ballard offered the following dedicatory prayer:

> Our Father, who art in Heaven, hallowed be Thy name. In the name of Jesus Christ, Thy Well Beloved Son, we Thy servants, approach Thee on this beautiful Christmas morning, in this secluded spot, in the City of Buenos Aires, Argentina South America; in a land far distant from our mountain home, but in a country which Thou hast called a part of the Land of Zion.

> We are very thankful for our safe arrival, after a voyage of twenty one days on the seas, without a moment's sickness. We do acknowledge that Thou didst temper the elements for our good, and that Thy protecting care has been over us in our travels, both upon the land and the sea, and for health and strength to labor for Thee and Thy cause.

We are grateful that we have been chosen by Thy servant, President Heber J. Grant, to come to this great land of South America, to unlock the door for the preaching of the Gospel, to all the peoples of the South American nations. To search out the blood of Israel that has been sifted among the Gentile nations, many of whom, influenced by the spirit of gathering, have assembled in this land.

Put Thy Spirit into their hearts, that they may receive us, as true messengers sent of God; for their Salvation. Help us to labor for them with the same Spirit in us, He had who loved men so that He died for them. That we may effectually "call, persuade, and invite" men to come unto Christ.

We thank Thee for the few who have received us, and for those we have had the joy of taking into the waters of baptism, in this land. May they be the first fruits of a glorious harvest.

We pray that we may have the opportunity to present to the people, the message which Thou hast sent us to deliver, namely; that angels, sent by Thee, have visited the earth, in this dispensation, bringing to men again the Everlasting Gospel. That John the Baptist did visit the Prophet Joseph Smith, upon whom he conferred, the authority to baptize.

That Peter, James, and John did ordain him, an apostle of the Lord Jesus Christ; and endow him with the keys of the Holy Priesthood with authority to baptize, with fire and the Holy Ghost; and to organize the Church of Jesus Christ again in the earth.

And that Moroni, Thine ancient Prophet of the Americas, did visit Joseph Smith, and deliver into his hands; the plates containing a history of the early inhabitants of this land. And that by Thy power, Joseph Smith did translate the characters on the plates, from which he obtained the Book of Mormon.

And that he was visited by Thee; and Thy Beloved Son, who committed into Joseph's hands, a great and new Gospel dispensation, for all flesh.

We are thankful that we are the bearers, of these glad tidings, to the peoples of the South American nations.

We also pray, that we may see, the beginning of the fulfillment of Thy promises, contained in the Book of Mormon, to the Indians of this land, who are descendants of Lehi; millions of whom reside in this country. Who have long been downtrodden, and born many afflictions, and suffered because of sin and transgression; even as the Prophets, of the Book of Mormon, did foretell. But Thou didst inspire, those Prophets, to promise their descendants that Thou wouldst bring forth in the latter-day, the records of the fathers. And that when these records, were presented to their children, they would begin to believe, and when they would do this, Thy favor would return unto them. And then Thou wouldst remember the promises made to their fathers; that if their descendants would repent, and receive the Gospel, they would begin to be prospered, and blessed on the land, and would again become a white and delightsome people.

O Father, let Thy Spirit work upon them, and manifest the truth of these things unto them, as we, and Thy servants, who shall follow us, shall bear witness, of Thy precious promises unto this branch of the House of Israel.

Father bless Thy Church, in all the earth; continue to guide those whom Thou hast called to lead it, with wisdom, and power to direct it forward to fulfill its great mission, in the earth.

Sustain Thy servants who labor as missionaries, in all parts of the world, that they may have the opportunity and power, to warn all men, that the hour of judgment approaches; and that Thou hast offered, through the Gospel, a means of escape for the calamities that shall come upon all flesh, unless they repent.

Remember in mercy, the "Hope of Israel", the youth of Thy Church, who are to bear the responsibilities of the future, that Thy may keep themselves clean, and undefiled, from the sins of the world; that they may be found worthy of their inheritance, and come to their glorious destiny. Bless those who are their shepherds, the watchmen upon the towers of Zion, that they may guard well the flock, and be able to feed, with the bread of life, the sheep and the lambs.

We present for Thy kind consideration, the members of our own families, from whom we are separated; who are now, and have in times past sacrificed much, that we may carry the Gospel to the children of men. May health and life attend each one, and the good cheer Thy Spirit brings, be with them, and above all, keep them from sin, and bless them with faith in Thee and Thy Gospel.

Bless the Presidents, governors and leading officials of these American countries, that they may kindly receive us, and give us permission to open the doors of salvation, to the peoples of these lands. may they be blessed in administering the affairs of their several offices, that great good may come unto the people. That peace may be upon these nations, that Thou hast made free, through Thy blessings upon the valiant liberators of these lands; the righteousness may obtain, and full liberty for the preaching of Thy Gospel prevail. Stay the power of evil that it shall not triumph over Thy work, but that all Thine enemies shall be subdued, and Thy truth be triumphant.

And now, O Father, by authority of the blessing and appointment, of Thy servant, the President of the Church, and by the authority of the Holy Apostleship, which I hold, I do turn the key, unlock and open the door, for the preaching of the Gospel, in all these South American nations; and do rebuke, and command to be stayed, every power that would oppose the preaching of the Gospel, in these lands. And we do bless, and dedicate these nations, and this land, for the preaching of the Gospel. And we do all this, that salvation may come, to all men, and that Thy name, may be honored and glorified in this part of the land of Zion.

Help us to bring men to Thee, and Thy Son, and speed the day, when He shall come, to rule as King of kings and Lord of lords. And for all Thy blessings, which shall bring success to our labors, we shall ascribe honor, and power and glory to Thee forever and ever. Amen.

The Brethren then sang, "Praise to the Man" after which each of the Brethren spoke briefly concerning their mission here, and their willingness to do their best to establish this mission; of their perfect love for each other, and the work of the Lord. They blessed each other, and felt that as the result of opening this mission, many Europeans in this land would receive the Gospel, but that ultimately, the great import of the mission would be to the Indians, and that this was a momentous day. A wonderful spirit was present, and all were visibly affected. Their joy was full and expressed in tears. At 4:00 p.m. that same day, they met with all of the German Saints at the home of Brother Friederichs, where they held a special Christmas program.

The weather continued to be excessively warm, and Brother Wells continued to be quite ill. On New Year's Eve, Brother Wells had the most violent attack of dizziness and vomiting he had yet suffered. He became so ill it was alarming to the others. His hands and feet were cold, and his head was cold with a cold sweat all over. The doctor diagnosed the cause of his dizziness was due to slight brain hemorrhages through hardening of the arteries. He recommended that he go back to his own country, to a higher elevation, and escape the terrific heat of this land. The Brethren sent a cablegram recommending the same. A short time later, they received a response from Salt Lake approving his return on the S.S. "American Legion" sailing January 14th.

In due time he reached home in safety, recovered, and lived for fifteen years. In fact, he outlived both of his companions on this mission. His illness and his forced return home were a deep disappointment to President Ballard and a great handicap to the missionary work. Rulon Wells spoke the German language fluently and was among the ablest expounders of the Gospel in his time. On Wednesday, January 6, 1926, they held a cottage meeting where there were ten Spanish speaking people present, and five Germans. On Wednesday, January 13, 1926, at 7:30 p.m., another Spanish and German meeting was held with sixteen Spanish speaking people and three German people present.

Some early obstacles arose when the announcement of the meetings failed to be printed in the "La Prensa" after it was promised to be done free of charge. Next, the release of their freight shipment of literature from Zion's Printing and Publishing Company, being a 1500 pound shipment of books and tracts, in English, German and Spanish, was denied owing to not having the original freight bills signed by the Argentina Consul of new Orleans. The "Nacion", another large paper, also promised to publish the meeting notice but likewise failed to do so. They had little hope of getting any help from the newspapers.

On Wednesday, January 27th, they held a Spanish and German meeting where there were fifty Spanish and six German speaking people present. Faith was strong and hopes were high. After weeks of search for a hall, wherein hundreds of places were visited, the Brethren decided to rent the quarters at 8968, 8970 and 8972 Rivadavia Street, consisting of front store room 24 x 36, for meeting purposes, and three good living rooms, with kitchen and bath, in the rear for $280.00 (pesos) per month. The Brethren bought some used furniture, in good condition, to fit up one room.

On Wednesday, March 24th, they sold one Book of Mormon. President Pratt, as for several weeks past, had spent the time translating hymns into Spanish. Elder Ballard would distribute between 250 - 500 of the new announcement tracts a day. Meetings began to have as many as a hundred present. On one occasion, they had a hundred children in their meeting. They were very hard to control. Having no idea of the sacredness of a meeting or what a Bible is or of its existence.

On Thursday, May 27th, Brother Ballard received a letter from the First Presidency stating that the missionaries for South America would leave New York on May 15th on the S.S. "Vandyke". Three weeks later, on Saturday, June 5th, they expected the missionaries from the United States on the boat that was reported to be in that night, but after waiting at the dock until 10:00 p.m., they were informed that on account of the fog, the boat would not arrive until the next day. On Sunday, June 6th, Brother Ballard went early to the dock to await the missionaries, but again, on account of the fog on the river, the boat did not get in until 3:00 p.m. At that hour he met

Elder Rienhold Stoof and his wife, Sister Ella Stoof, and Elders Vernon Sharp and Waldo Stoddard, and brought them to the mission house.

At 5:00 p.m., the regular Sacrament and testimony meeting was held in the meeting hall. All the missionaries spoke, and Elder Stoof interpreted for those who could not speak German. At 7:30 p.m., a Spanish meeting was held in the hall with thirty present. Elder Sharp spoke first and was followed by Brother Pratt. After the meeting, Brother Ballard sent a cable to President Grant informing him that the missionaries all arrived well.

A week later, the Elders went to the Y.M.C.A. and saw the Secretary and applied for a tank to baptize in, but they were refused. So, they went to the place where Elder Ballard baptized the German converts shortly after arriving in South America and held the baptism of Mrs. Eladia Sifuentes. She was then confirmed on the riverbank. Others mentioned who made progress were the Florencio Gonzales family and Senora Molares.

On Tuesday, June 29th, Brother Ballard wrote to the First Presidency advising them that he and President Rey L. Pratt expected to leave Buenos Aires for home, going by way of the West Coast, on July 23, 1926. On Monday, July 12th, Brothers Ballard and Pratt went to town and learned at the railroad office that the road over the Andes to Valpariso was blocked with snow and would likely not be open until September. They, therefore, began to plan their return journey by way of Tucuman, La Quiaca and La Paz, Bolivia.

One interested person, Dr. A.S. Ossorio, called at Elders' rooms at 10:30 p.m. and talked with Brother Pratt until after midnight. He again said he wished to be baptized and join the Church. Brother Pratt explained all that that meant and assured the doctor that we had nothing to offer him that was not offered to the most humble. He manifested that he had faith in the Gospel as restored and was willing to accept on the conditions named, and still wished to be baptized. It was agreed that his baptism should take place soon.

Elders Ballard and Pratt were very grateful after many months of hard work, often in the midst of great discouragement, to see the work so well established. The openings in both the German and Spanish parts of it, being so favorable with a large number of people interested, with many places opened for meetings, and several investigators who have already indicated that they expect to be baptized. They also met with some Italians. They wrote, on Wednesday, July 14th, "We see no reason why, with the Lord's help, building on this good foundation, the missionaries cannot succeed in establishing a flourishing mission of the Church in South America. And we leave with the feeling that we have done our duty and that the Lord has blessed and accepted our efforts, and that we have accomplished the purpose for which we were sent."

After a farewell meeting, with the people feeling very regretful that the Brethren must leave, Brother Ballard found a notice that he had a telegram awaiting him downtown. Upon securing it, he found that it was the permission from the First Presidency to return by way of the West Coast. So on Friday, July 23rd, all arose early to prepare for the departure of Elders Ballard and Pratt. They left from the Retiro Station for Rosario at 10 o'clock. Dr. Ossorio accompanied them and the Brethren to the station. Mrs. Ballard was at the wharf in New York to welcome her husband. On the way home they visited Niagara Falls, Palmyra, the Hill Cumorah, the Sacred Grove, and slept in the Smith home.

Elder Ballard came home with a firsthand knowledge of South America and its people. He had journeyed up to the headwaters of the Amazon River and over the Andes Mountains, observing the high, broad plateaus of those mountains covered with small farms, occupied by industrious, peace-loving native Indians, of whom he saw thousands engaged in raising barley, corn, potatoes, cattle and sheep. He was favorably impressed with the native people, whom he did not doubt were descendants of Lehi, and with ancient ruins in South America which confirm the story of the Book of Mormon.

He had spent over seven months in South America and had been ten months away from home on this mission. The brethren had encountered many obstacles -- hot, humid weather, roads made almost impassable by heavy rains, press opposition, the people's indifference toward religion. But none of these obstacles, nor all of them combined, could deter Elder Ballard. Though personally handicapped by lack of the German or Spanish languages and the consequent need to use interpreters, he pressed on with patience, tolerance and a prayerful heart. The efforts he and his associates made paid off, for they resulted in a small but secure beginning for the Lord's work in that great continent.

The pre-natal promise and patriarchal blessing received further fulfillment in this mission. "In the midst of Zion," of which South America is a part, he proved to be a "mighty prophet" again, not only in proclaiming his great witness to the divine Sonship of Jesus Christ, but also in the demanding predictive role. For at a testimony meeting held in Buenos Aires on July 4, 1926, Elder Ballard made this prophecy, which Elder Vernon Sharp recorded in his missionary diary on pages 83-84:

> The work of the Lord will grow slowly for a time here just as an oak grows slowly from an acorn. It will not shoot up in a day as does the sunflower that grows quickly and then dies. But thousands will join the Church here. It will be divided into more than one mission and will be one of the strongest in the Church. The work here is the smallest that it will ever be. The day will come when the Lamanites in this land will be

given a chance. The South American Mission will be a power in the Church. And "the end is not yet."

Several months later, President Reinhold Stoof wrote an article that appeared in the Improvement Era 31 (October 1928): 1052-1054. "It has seldom been easy to introduce the Gospel into a new country . . ." "Hard labor in a new soil! Many, very many weeds in it! But, fortunately, weeds serve a good purpose. They keep the gardener's back lithe and will not allow him the luxury of resting too much. There are plenty of weeds to remove in this field before our gardeners can reach good soil. One finds but little prejudice against our Church; but ignorance of the Bible and indifference in religious matters are the main obstacles which must be overcome. Neither must one forget that 32% of the population are illiterates in Argentina and that a Bible is very seldom found in a house . . ."

"But the missionaries were soon to discover that among the Latin people as many good and honest souls are to be found as among the peoples of Europe . . . We do believe that here, too, every faithful missionary will reap the fruits of his diligent labors and will richly enjoy the blessings of our Heavenly Father in his work."

"The whole mission consists now of sixty-five members; five of whom live in Southern Brazil . . . Thirteen blest children are included in the membership. Thirty-one are of German, twenty of Argentine, seven of Italian, five of Spanish, one of Irish, and one of Yugoslavian nationality. . . "
"We extend a hearty welcome to all missionaries who will join us in our labors. We need them. There is so much work before us . . ."

Brother Ballard implored in his prayer of dedication the blessings of the Almighty God upon the descendants of Lehi, the Indians of this continent. Indicating that millions of them live here, downtrodden, in a state of semi-slavery. The

Gospel of Jesus Christ will redeem them from much of their misery . . . Youth of Zion, here is something that should appeal to you! Come with all your talents and power, where the hardest problems are to be solved, right here in SOUTH AMERICA!

The article was concluded by the following quote from Brigham Young. "When you read the revelations, or when you hear the will of the Lord concerning you, for your own sakes never receive that with a doubtful heart."

Chapter 3

Missionary Moments

Elder James Vernon Sharp was one of the first full-time missionaries to arrive in South America. He recorded the following: "We arrived in Buenos Aires on June 8, 1926. This was a Sunday. We had something happen that Sunday that was the highlight of Brother Stoof's life and inasmuch as there are only two of us alive who were present at that time -- Brother Waldo I. Stoddard and myself -- I think it would be well to tell of the gift of tongues that was enjoyed by Brother Reinhold Stoof who had been called to be president of the South American Mission. He knew no Spanish, absolutely no Spanish, even a year after he had been there. He was interested in working with the German people, he did not study Spanish, he did not try to ever conjugate a verb. He would use it in the infinitive and say "They would know how to conjugate it better than I do."

"We had been all these long days on the sea coming up the La Plata River and were supposed to disembark early on this Sunday the 8th, but a fog came up and the boat became stuck in the mud on the Rio de La Plata. Apostle Ballard was waiting for us all of this time until the boat docked. Brother Ballard was there as we came through customs. We didn't bother to get our trunks or anything because there was a meeting behind held at 8968 Rivadavia Street. He wanted to get us out to it in time . . .

"The mission was opened in South America at that time primarily to reach the German Saints, because there were three or four families of German Saints who had migrated there and at their request the mission had been opened. The majority of the members talked German. There were also several folks who talked Spanish who were investigators, and so out of deference to the country it was decided by the Brethren at the commencement of this meeting that I should talk first in Spanish, which I did. I was asked to relate missionary experiences in Mexico. President Rey L. Pratt was to relate missionary experiences in English as I spoke to President Stoof who at the termination of my talk was to give a resume in German so that the German Saints could understand what I had said. As I began to talk President Stoof said to President Pratt, "There's no need for you to tell me in English what Brother Sharp is saying in Spanish because I understand every word." Now Brother Stoof <u>never</u> became proficient in Spanish, but that day he enjoyed the gift of tongues. As I talked in Spanish he understood every word I said. When I sat down he directly translated it into German to the German Saints there without having it translated from Spanish to English. That was one of the highlights in his life and in our lives, of course.

"In Matthew 19:14 Jesus said, 'Suffer little children, and forbid them not, to come unto me: for of such is the Kingdom of Heaven.' So often we expect the great changes or miracles and inventions to come from the wise and learned. We expect to bring the parents of families into the Church, but often they are brought in by their children. Speaking of the birth of the Church in South America, Brother Sharp explained this when he said on page 8: '. . . We could get nowhere trying to preach the Gospel in Spanish, and the German people who had migrated there who were not members of the Church were not interested and so here we were up against a stone wall . . . it was decided that we should start with Sunday Schools in the homes of these German Saints, but conduct Spanish Sunday Schools and invite the neighbors because the children, the young folks, seemed to be interested. And so it was by means of the Sunday School that we were able to get the work started in South America.'

"Elder Ray L. Pratt was a master of tongue and pen. He was a poet in English; he was a poet in Spanish. He translated many of the hymns and helped publish a small hymn book called <u>Himnos de Sion</u>. There I learned that the apostles and members of the Council of the Seventy were human even as you and I. We had one boy that was a monotone. He couldn't sing a tune. He just had one note and he could drown out anybody else in the audience. Now Brother Ballard and Brother Pratt were both musicians and one Sunday this boy -- his name was Pedro Peter -- was absent at our little Sunday School. Brother Ballard said, 'Well, I'm going to miss Foghorn Peter.' So, I found that he was human.

On another occasion "We were told of a shortcut one dark winter night, so that we wouldn't have to walk so far from where we were holding these cottage meetings . . . it was raining. Instead of going one direction, if we went in another we could get a streetcar sooner. So we went to that and as we were walking along, President Pratt, with his hands in his pockets, slipped. He couldn't get his hands out of his pockets before he fell with his face in the mud and he said, "If I ever do anything those damn Germans tell me to again, I hope I die." So I knew from those two reactions that dedicated as they were, they were human. By the way, this shortcut proved to be the long way round. It took us a good hour longer than the other way would have taken us.

"The first Spanish-speaking convert was a Sister Eladia Sifuentes. She was baptized on June 6, 1926, by President Rey L. Pratt in the La Plata River. She was a very valuable asset to the Church in its early days, but it turned out that she was, as you might say, a professional joiner. She joined everything that came along and after a while she left the Church."

Louis G. Tremelling wrote that "the neighborhood of Velez Sarfield was tracted and invitations to see free movie slides of Salt Lake and the Mormons were distributed. One of these tract invitations was left at the neat small home of Carmen Montes Escudero and her daughter, Isabel. They went because the movie slides were free and they were curious about the Mormons. About 200 people attended. The slides were projected on the wall of the old laundry building. Rey L. Pratt, who spoke Spanish fluently, was the narrator and with a long wooden pointer explained the message of the slides. As both the Escudero women were musically talented, the thing which impressed them most was: To one side and near the front sat Melvin J. Ballard on a raised platform playing a small portable organ, singing the hymns in English. They were so thrilled and inspired by Elder Ballard's flowing white hair and the music he made that they remarked, "He must be a man of God or a Saint." They attended the remainder of the meetings until Elders Ballard and Pratt left Argentina. To the best of their knowledge, they were among the only ones attending these first meetings who embraced the Gospel.

"Hermana Escudero, as she was fondly called by many missionaries, declared that she owed them a great debt of gratitude for having brought the Gospel into her home. In order to partly pay this debt she washed the missionaries clothes on a washboard without accepting any pay for it for 16 years, or as long as her health would permit. Later she became the first president of the Relief Society in the first branch established. She was a teacher in the Sunday School and helped the missionaries open other branches in the city. In 1955, she came to the United States where she went through the temple in Mesa, Arizona and had her deceased husband sealed to her. After many devoted and faithful years to the missionary cause she died September 8, 1968.

"When her daughter, Isabel, received her patriarchal blessing she was told: 'The Lord has a great work in store for you. You are to be a Savior unto your people. You are a natural missionary. You have a gift in this direction. Use it and the Lord will bless the labors of your hand.'

"When Isabel was 14 years old she was leading the singing in her branch. Later she was called as a local missionary and tracted in the streets of Buenos Aires at the age of 17. She sang in the Church choirs and the mission quartet, which traveled about the mission. In 1938 she married Louis G. Tremelling and came to Logan, Utah and later moved to Monterrey, Mexico.

"When the family returned to the United States she helped establish a Sunday School and fellowshiped the Spanish-speaking members in the Idaho Falls, Idaho area. In 1977 she and her husband filled a mission in Osorno, Chile and then spent most of their time furthering the Spanish extraction program." She was engaged in missionary work for more than forty years.

Elder Sharp recorded that "There was a little Italian girl by the name of Rosa, about eight years of age. A little blond Italian, and she came to me one day and she said, "Brother Sharp, my folks will not let me come to Sunday School." And I said, "Well, that's too bad, but I see you at Sunday School all the time. How come?" She said, "I go to the home of my aunt with my little brother, and my aunt washes our faces and combs our hair, and we come to Sunday School with our cousins." I said, "Rosa, we surely want you to be at Sunday School, but first of all you must do what your parents say. That's the first thing and someday they'll let you come to Sunday School." She said, fine, she would do that. Now we noticed that she continued to come to Sunday School with her little brother.

She became very ill in September with diphtheria and measles combined. She became unconscious the fore part of the week. On a Friday, she aroused and on Friday we had the habit of holding a cottage meeting in Liniers, the area in which she lived. She became unconscious, as I said, the fore part of the week and on Friday roused up and said to her mother, "What day is today?" Her mother said, "Friday." Rosa said, "Oh my, there's a meeting and if I don't take some flowers to the missionaries, they're going to wonder what's wrong." With those words she passed away.

It made quite an impression upon the parents that the last thought of their little girl should be of the missionaries. We found that the people were poor, and they couldn't afford a funeral because the church to which they belonged, the Catholic Church, would charge them for a funeral. So we immediately contacted them through our friends and told them that we would be happy, free of charge, to hold a funeral. They said they would love that, so Elder Stoddard and I went out. We helped them get a coffin, and held a funeral service for little Rosa.

That had a profound effect in the neighborhood, that here were people that loved their people so much that we'd come out and hold a funeral where the members of their own church would have to have money for it. It made such an impression that it helped convert some people.

Elder Sharp continued, "Then there was the first family that joined the Church in South America. In Liniers, just around the corner from where little Rosa lived, was the home of Donato Gianfelice, where lived his wife, their children and a fellow Italian by the name of Domingo Quicci. One day Apostle Ballard and President Rey L. Pratt were tracting. They couldn't get into the house because there was a fence in front. They clapped their hands which is what you did to get the people's attention, but there was nobody home, so they left a tract at the gate.

"The Gianfelices became interested in the Church. Both Domingo Quicci and Donato Gianfelice were ditch diggers and made very little money. However, when they got their pay each weekend, they would go to the local saloon and drink up their wages. When they came back to the house, they had no money for food for the following week. Now some thieves in the neighborhood took note of what happened. So one day when they had gotten their paycheck, before they got to the saloon, they were beaten up and left half-dead and the money was taken. When they came home from the hospital to convalesce, neither one of them could read, but Sister Gianfelice could read -- at that time not a member of the Church, of course. The only material to read that they had in the house was the tract that had been left by Apostle Ballard and Rey L. Pratt. So she read and reread this tract which was <u>A Friendly Discussion</u> by Ben E. Rich.

"After Brother Ballard and Brother Pratt left, Brother Stoddard and myself went to continue to visit with them. And they became more and more interested in the Gospel, but they were being visited by Seventh Day Adventist missionaries, and they couldn't make up their minds which was the true Church. The Seventh Day Adventist missionaries said, "Well, let's have a debate between us and the Mormon missionaries." So when Brother Gianfelice and Domingo Quicci came to us about a debate we said, "Well, nothing's gained by a debate. We don't debate on religious things; they're either right or they're wrong, and the spirit of the Lord will let you know whether it's right or wrong." So they took that message to the Seventh Day Adventist missionary and he said, "Oh, they're scared of us." So we got the message back and talked about it with President Stoof and he said, "Well, rather than lose our only investigators, we'd better bend a rule and have a debate. What do they want to debate on?" Well, the first thing they wanted to debate on was the Sabbath and, of course, in Spanish it's <u>Sabado</u> (Saturday). The Seventh Day Adventists thought that if they had a debate on the Sabbath they'd win. So we talked to Donato Gianfelice, and we set up a time for a debate and he went to the Seventh Day Adventist missionaries and said, "All right, the debate can be any time you want, any place you want." And the Seventh Day Adventist missionary said, "I'll bet you five pesos we win."

"Donato Gianfelice said, "Look, this is serious business. You don't bet about it, and there won't be any debate, I've decided already." So we held no debate. They were baptized. At that time as I said, neither one of them could read or write. Brother Gianfelice learned to read by reading the Book of Mormon. The day that he was baptized he said, "The most precious thing in my life is the Gospel and that which it means to me. If I should ever lose my testimony or commence to lose it, I would rather die, I value it more than my life." And to the day that he died, he was most faithful. Brother Waldo Stoddard and myself baptized the family. He had a son, Antonio, who was too young to be baptized at that time, but later on Antonio became the patriarch of the first stake when it was formed in Argentina. This all directly goes back into the neighborhood where little Rosa passed away, and her funeral so impressed the people that we were able to influence these folks and that was the real beginning of the missionary work in the area. Also, with the young folks in Sunday Schools in South America, particularly in Buenos Aires.

Brother Sharp recorded Elder Ballard as saying that he had talked with Jesus Christ and had seen him and knew that he lives as much as he will every know anything. Also to Brother Ballard has been revealed many things that will happen in the future and they have done so. He has healed the sick in cases too numerous to mention, bringing them back, as it were, from the very jaws of death. . . he told us after the meeting that there were some of us that would live to see the fulfillment of those words and, of course, I was there. But truly the work did go slowly at first.

During the last months of his mission, Elder Sharp traveled to Bolivia to investigate the possibilities of working there. He soon found himself in the middle of a revolution and later received his honorable release and instructions to go home. He writes the following of his travels from Bolivia through Peru: "On June 4th I received word from Reinhold Stoof that I had been honorably released and should proceed on home. So on June 4th I left for home, crossed Lake Titicaca to Puno. By the way, I crossed steerage at night. It snowed on us. We had no cover overhead and we arrived at Puno. Then I went on up to Cuzco and to Ollantytambu saw the ruins there, and could go no farther because the construction train went only that far. Then I went on to Arequipa, spent two days there, and then on to Mollendo, Peru. There I boarded the boat to go to the United States. A very interesting thing happened in Mollendo. I had twenty-four hours in Mollendo before boarding the boat. There was a meeting being held in a Protestant church, and I went there to see what they were doing and lo and behold I saw a tract called A Voice of Warning, one of our Mormon tracts. It had been left the year before by President Pratt and Brother Ballard, and they had told these people that later on missionaries would come to Mollendo, Peru, and that they would bring the true Gospel to them. These people were unhappy with their pastor and had discharged him. They had no leader at the time that I went through. I said, 'Well, I'm not the leader, but sometime later you will have missionaries in this city, I assure you.' Many, many years later as we'll find as we go on with this narrative, it was my privilege to take missionaries into Mollendo when I was mission president.

"I went on up from Mollendo to Lima, Peru, then from Lima to the Panama Canal. I changed to a fruit boat in Panama, went on to New Orleans and arrived there on the Fourth of July. I came up the Mississippi River, met a cousin of mine, and we came to some street meetings. Then I came on home arriving right around the twenty-fourth of July, finishing that portion of the mission."

The seeds had been planted and some had begun to sprout, grow and bear fruit. One of the missionary moments significant to the history of the church in Peru occurred more than ten years after the first missionaries had begun preaching the gospel in Argentina. It was later recorded in the Church News and described a scene where Elder Louis G. Tremelling and his companion couldn't find a seat aboard a noisy bus in Buenos Aries:

As the missionaries stood near the door, Elder Tremelling watched a tall, young man with an athletic build dispense bus tickets. He had a money bag, ticket dispenser and a notebook attached to a clipboard for keeping a record of each transaction.

"All at once I could see he was in trouble," Elder Tremelling recalled. As he moved up for a closer look, the elder heard the young man say he had lost his pencil and would lose his job unless he kept an accurate record of his transactions.

"I do not know what impelled me to reach in my pocket and give him my new pen -- which I had just purchased that day," Elder Tremelling said. He handed the pen to the ticket-taker, explaining, "You need it more than I do."

"Who are you?" the young man asked. The Americans told him they were missionaries from The Church of Jesus Christ of Latter-day Saints. "Where do you live?" The missionaries said they lived in Haedo, a small town outside of Buenos Aires.

"I live there, too," replied the young man. Two days later, the ticket-taker found the missionaries' residence and returned the pen. His name was Samuel Boren. Before he could leave, the missionaries asked him if he would allow them to visit his home and teach him and his family the restored Gospel.

"You surely can," he said without hesitation. Three weeks later, on September 12, 1936, he and his parents and family were baptized. Shortly after his baptism, Boren served a mission in Argentina. Later, he married Clara Angela Lorenzi. He would later become a successful building manager for the Church in South America and for business interests in

America. Since joining the Church, Boren has served as a mission president in Mexico and twice in Italy. He also has been a regional representative and was called as president of the Lima, Peru, Temple.

Among those called as officiators at the temple were Louis and Isabel Tremelling from Idaho Falls, Idaho.

Peru would wait a little longer for the light of the Gospel to be sent to fulfill the promises made by the Lord to the descendants of Lehi.

Chapter 4
(Summary of Chapter IX)
From An Acorn To An Oak:
A Personal History of the Establishment and First Quarter Century Development of the South American Mission
Fullerton: Etcetera Etcetera Graphics, 1987
By Frederick S. Williams and Frederick G. Williams

PERU: THE DAWNING OF THE DAY OF THE LAMANITES (1956-1959)

Many Latter-day Saints have lived at different times in Peru, and have contributed to the development of the country. The Cerro de Pasco copper mine was consolidated and developed by a member of the Church, Brother A/W. McCune. He brought several young Latter-day Saints to work with him in Peru. Chauncey Spilbury came as the tutor of the McCune children. Chauncey's younger brother came to work with the company and became manager, serving in this capacity for many years.

Stanley A. Moore, a former Argentine missionary, came to Peru in 1943 to work for Panagra as a radio engineer. Except for two years, he resided in Peru continuously with his wife, Edna Zaldivar, and their four children, all born in Lima, until the 1960s. They held Sunday Schools in their home during their sojourn. Other families had come and gone: John Alius, a United Press correspondent, Eugene Turley, from Phoenix, Arizona, an advertising executive, Quintin West, an agronomist serving with the world food production organization.

In February 1954, President and Sister David O. McKay and their son Robert Riggs McKay, visited Lima and a special meeting was held. After the meeting President McKay discussed with the priesthood holders the possibilities of establishing a mission in Peru. President McKay planned to research Peruvian law to see if a mission could be legally established.

Frederick S. Williams had arrived with his wife Corraine, son Frederick G., and daughters Nancy Lou and Mary, to establish a home and an import/expert business in that country. Colonel Charles H. Shaw, U.S. Air Attache, and his family in February; the Wells Allred family in March, a marketing specialist with the World Food Production Organization. Ana Gloria Giustra was contacted. She had attended church in New York. Other Latter-day Saint families connected with the Southern Peru Copper Mines, like the Warren Smiths, of Cerro de Pasco, and the Kay W. Footes, also came.

On April 16, 1956, Brother Williams wrote to the First Presidency expressing the hope that Elder Henry D. Moyle, who was scheduled to visit the South American missions in May, could organize them officially. With 28 members from the U.S. he explained,

"Our problem is that we have no organization. We belong to no mission. Our recommends are scattered throughout the Church. The former group leader, Brother Turley, has been gone from Peru for over a year . . . I feel that a mission could very advantageously be established in Peru. It would take time for us to get well established as the Catholic Church is very strong and would fight us with every facility at their command. There are thousands of good people who are not satisfied with what they have, and I am sure that many would join the Church if they were given an opportunity."

On February the 29, 1956, Brother Williams wrote President Franklin D. Parry of the Uruguayan Mission, "I trust that someday missionaries may be sent here. There are many of the descendants of father Lehi whom I feel would accept the message of the restored Gospel of the Savior." On April the

17, President Frank D. Parry of the Uruguayan Mission wrote me back,

> "We have received communications from the First Presidency authorizing the establishment of a branch under the Uruguayan Mission at Lima, Peru. We also have received permission to send two missionaries into that city to work towards the end of establishing permanent missionary work in that country. Endeavoring to secure permits from the proper authorities to begin missionary work, it was recommended that the American Ambassador in Lima introduce Elder Henry D. Moyle to the Foreign Minister during his visit to Lima. Brother Moyle would at that time present an official application for permission to carry out our missionary programs. . . (It was Brother Williams) opinion that missionaries not be sent to Peru until after Elder Moyle's visit so missionary work could begin with the permission of the government."

Brother Williams again wrote to President Parry explaining that "By the constitution we are permitted to work here, but they can beat us by choking off our missionary supply -- just let the applications lie in a basket without attention. A permanent visa can only be granted from Lima and it takes a long time at best." President Parry agreed and Elder Moyle made his schedule available.

Brother Williams describes the Lima Branch being organized. "Elder Henry D. Moyle and wife arrived in Lima on July 6, 1956; President Frank D. Parry and daughter Sharon had arrived the day before. (Sister Parry, the President's wife, had recently passed away, but he continued to preside over the mission without her, often traveling accompanied by his daughter.) We made reservations for the Moyle's at the Crillon Hotel. We visited with them Friday night, picnicked Saturday, and Sunday morning held Sunday School in our home on Avenida La Paz. This was a joyous occasion, the house was completely filled with people. Our little makeshift chapel contained equally makeshift benches made of boards covered with folded blankets placed between chairs; thus six or seven people could avail themselves of the space provided by two chairs. We held classes in bedrooms and in the backyard. We had been holding Sunday School and Sacrament meeting for several months, but this was a wonderful opportunity to partake of the sacrament in the presence of an Apostle and President Parry. Twenty-seven people attended that day.

"After Church, we invited our guests to dinner at our home and then that night, a special meeting was held in the home of Colonel Charles Howard Shaw, the American Air Attache, on Avenida Javier Prado and 320 Los Cedros. During the meeting, attended by thirty people, the Shaws, the Moores, the Allreds and the Williams, together with Ana Gloria Giustra and two returning Argentine missionaries, all bore testimony of the restored Gospel. A trio, my wife, son Fred and daughter Nancy, sang "The Bridge Builder." That evening, July 8, 1956, the Lima Branch was organized. Elder Moyle set me apart as Branch President, the first in Peru, with Stanley A. Moore as first counselor, Charles H. Shaw as counselor, and my son Fred G. Williams as secretary. Apostle Moyle spoke prophetic words about the future of the work in this country and invoked the Lord's blessings on the branch and its members.

On Monday, they had their interview with the Minister of Justice and Religion in Charge of Foreign Affairs, General Felix Huaman, Brother Moyle, a seasoned attorney as well as General Authority, eloquently explained the purpose of our visit. The interview lasted forty-five minutes, and they left with the necessary information to gain permission to do work in Peru. They then drafted a formal petition to the Peruvian government."

On one occasion the Williams invited the Moyle's for potluck supper. Elder Moyle replied, "Would I? I'd be tickled to death. Why I've even been eating corn flakes in the hotel room with mineral water, I was afraid of the milk." After the meal, Brother Moyle said, "That's the best meal I have had since I left home. Everywhere I go, the people try to kill me with kindness and goodness and prepare big meals; something like this is just wonderful."

Arriving August 3, 1956, Elder Darwin Thomas and Elder Sherl Plowman became the first missionaries to labor in Peru. Generally speaking, the Mission President in Uruguay would send missionaries who had four or five months to go to complete their missions. There were four and sometimes six missionaries working in Lima. In the beginning, the Williams home was their headquarters; later they lived in *pensiones*.

The building, at 1210 Avenida Orrantia in San Isidro, Lima, was a beautiful three story tudor home and was the first piece of property owned by the Church in Peru and served as a chapel and later became the headquarters of the Andean Mission when organized November 1, 1959. The large living-dining room was adequate for a chapel, the sun porch was curtained by the Relief Society sisters to make a room for a small kindergarten children class, and the four upstairs bedrooms became classrooms.

Under the authority of the First Presidency, Brother Williams requested the *Personeria Juridica* for the Church in Peru or, in other words, the official recognition of the Church as an official entity within the confines of Peru. With the aid of an attorney, Dr. Manuel Garcia Calderon, they were able to prepare all the papers and then present them to the proper ministry.

After many, many months and after numerous visits to the ministry, an investigator came out to the home and said he was checking the request, and said that he wanted to know more about the Church. Brother Williams took him by car, and together they went over to visit the chapel. The investigator was told,

"There's a better way that you can find out what kind of people we are, here's our schedule of meetings, we hold Sunday School at this time, and Church at such and such a time, and Mutual on Tuesday nights, at this hour, why don't you just come. Investigators are coming all the time, and friends; you could just see what is going on. We won't be putting on a front for you, they won't know who you are."

He said, "I think I'd just like to do that, you might be surprised to see me out there some day." He never did come, but perhaps some other investigator from the government may have come. A few months later the recognition was granted, and the Church was legally and lawfully constituted and officially recognized to work within the national territory of Peru.

Brother Williams continued, "One of our early converts was the most famous folk singer of Peru, Luis Abanto Morales. He was a radio personality and made records which sold throughout Peru. His voice could always be heard on the local radio, and it was wonderful to have him come on a Tuesday night -- we'd tell him that we were going to have a little fiesta that night at Mutual -- and he would come directly from the radio station, and bring with him whatever musicians there might be there at the time. One night he brought the accompanist for Ima Sumac; she was indisposed, but had planned to come; she had appeared briefly on the radio and then gone to her home.

"All this time we were having problems getting permanent visas for missionaries: hence only missionaries who were practically through with their missions in Uruguay were eligible to come into Peru. In one way this was good, because for the most part they were mature missionaries, all of them speaking fluent Spanish.

"When I applied for a visa to go to Peru, after a short visit there and after consulting an attorney who had a friend in the agency who granted visas (I made my application to the

Peruvian Consulate in Los Angeles), it took a little better than two months. Making application for these permanent visas for the full-time missionaries coming to Peru from Uruguay, I found that most of the elders had practically finished their missions before they were received. I presented the request in the name of the Uruguayan Mission in Lima, but we were getting nowhere. We knew that if we were going to have a fully constituted mission, we would have to get better service on visas; but this was rather difficult under the Peruvian law. It seems that the Lord prepares ways, so that His purposes can be performed, and here is rather an interesting sidelight on how this particular problem was solved.

"The missionaries were instrumental in baptizing a very lovely girl by the name of Elba Coloma who spoke some English and, being enthused with what the missionaries had told her about Brigham Young University, had decided to go to school in Provo. She requested admittance to the University; we sent up her papers and eventually she was accepted by the department, but the Office of Admissions had not yet sent the official letter of acceptance to her, which she needed to obtain her visa from the American Consulate. She wanted to go up a few months early to live with her uncle who lived in San Francisco and perfect her English before school started. Time went on and soon it was impossible for her to do that because no visa was forthcoming. In desperation, just a few days before classes were to start, I sent rather a nasty telegram to President Wilkinson. In it I reiterated the entire history, how she had been accepted, but still lacked the official notification from the University that she was a full-time student and therefore could not obtain a visa. I added that this was very poor public relations for the United States and especially for The Church of Jesus Christ of Latter-day Saints.

"Well, the telegram got results. The next day she received a phone call from the Consul, in which he explained that they had received a cable from BYU and that she could now pick up her visa, which she did and immediately left for the United States, arriving just in time to begin the Fall 1958 term.

"It so happened that Elba Coloma's uncle was the man in charge of visas for the Peruvian government, and he was very much interested in his niece. He told Elba's mother that if there was anything that he could ever do to help me -- since I had been kind to go to bat for his niece -- to be sure to call on him. Remembering our problems with visas, I promptly went to see him, and told him what the situation was regarding our missionaries. He said, "Leave it up to me, I'll see what I can do to help you. When you want a new visa, come and see me personally."

"The most dramatic example of his help came a year later. I believe that it was the month of August when we received the word that the Andean Mission was to be organized and that J. Vernon Sharp would be the mission president. Whatever date that was, I received a cablegram from the First Presidency stating that President and Sister Sharp had left Salt Lake City for New York where they would embark on one of the Grace Line steamers for Lima, Peru, some five days hence, and would I kindly secure a permanent visa for them and have it cabled to the Peruvian Consulate in New York.

"I remembered back to the two months that it had taken me to get a permanent visa for Peru and the trouble we had had getting visas for the missionaries; then I remembered my friend Mr. Coloma down in the Foreign Ministry. I went down at ten o'clock when the office opened, and told him my problem and he said, "Would five o'clock be too late for this afternoon?" I said, "No, that would be wonderful." "Well come back and see me at five." I returned at five o'clock in the afternoon and the visas were ready in the form of a cable, which I sent to New York to the Peruvian Consulate, and another copy to the First Presidency stating that the permanent visas were ready. I don't think the First Presidency ever did realize the problem that we'd had in gaining a permanent visa for anyone; they just requested that it be done, and fortunately it was done. I don't believe the Church has ever had any problem getting permanent visas and getting them immediately from the Peruvian government since that time. When in Peru in August 1967, I found that Mr. Coloma had died; but he had set up the procedure and established the machinery to service the missionaries, and it had been going on every since. Without this great service, it would have been impossible to establish the mission on the basis that it is, because it would have taken so many months to get visas, and as the Church members know, the missionaries don't know that far in advance where they are going.

Elder Harold B. Lee visited Cuzco, a city located 11,400 feet above sea level. Quite a few of the tourists got *Serroche*, or altitude sickness. Nevertheless, the party enjoyed a wonderful trip down the Urubamba Valley, held sacred by the Incas. Referring to the organization of the Andes Mission on Sunday, November 1, 1959 by Elder Lee, brother Williams indicated that some of his statements were quite prophetic. While in Brother Lee's office in Salt Lake City, he recalled that occasion and said, "You know, in thinking over what I said, I certainly spoke of things that were beyond my knowledge. I think that they must have been prophetic and under the inspiration of the Lord." The first Cancion de la Mision de Los Andes, words by Frederick S. Williams.

La Mision de Los Andes,
   La Mision amada, la recien llegada a la America del Sud.
La Mision de Los Andes,
   Obra tan divina que a todos nos ensena el amor y la virtud.
La Mision de Los Andes, te damos nuestro amor
   dando gracias al Senor.
En el cielo los angeles se ven complacidos al ver el comienzo
   de la obra el Salvador.

Translated, this beautiful song describes "the beloved Andes Mission recently come to South America. This work so divine that to all we teach love and virtue. To you Lord, we give our love and gratitude. In the heavens the angels rejoice in the commencement of the work of the Lord." Indeed, all of heaven rejoiced as the anxiously awaited work commenced in this great land of Peru which held the promise, along with others, to bless all the families of the earth.

Chapter 5

The Andes Mission

On April 9, 1956, The First Presidency authorized President Frank D. Parry (Calle Brito del Pino 1525, Montevideo, Uruguay) to send missionaries into Peru. This letter is made a part of this history:

> Dear Brother Parry: We have your letter of February 6 which you advise us that Brother Frederick S. Williams has informed you of his new position and residence in Lima, Peru, and that he had asked: "How could we arrange to have our little Mormon group come under the Uruguayan Mission?" We note that there are two families with ten members in each family.
>
> We recommend that you send two competent missionaries to Lima, who, with Brother Williams' assistance, should endeavor to secure permission from the proper authorities to begin missionary work. It would seem desirable, and we hope it will be feasible, to contact the Mayor of the city and government officials in higher positions to acquaint them with the nature of our work and its record of accomplishment in other areas. It would be ascertained whether or not recognition of the Church by registration or otherwise is essential, and how it may be accomplished. Of course, it will be necessary to secure quarters for the missionaries. Brother Williams will be of value in this effort.
>
> You are authorized to consider Lima as a Branch of your Mission, and to treat it as such in your administration and reports. As the residence of Brother Williams is sufficiently permanent, it is assumed that you would wish to make him Branch president; the first steps are to

contact the authorities and arrange for the beginning of missionary service. We think perhaps with one so experienced as Brother Williams you can attend to the initial steps by correspondence. It may be necessary later for you personally to visit in Lima. Since the trip from Montevideo to Lima may be rather expensive, we authorize you to charge the transportation of the missionaries to that point against the operations of the mission. After you have made investigation, we shall be pleased to have you report. You are at liberty to write Brother Williams before sending the missionaries if you think it desirable to do so.

On August 7, 1956, the first missionaries assigned to the Peruvian District were as follows: Edward T. Hall (who was First District President), Donald L. Hokanson and Shirrel M. Plowman. Three months later on November 30, 1956, the property at 1210 Orrantia Avenue, San Isidro, in Lima, Peru was purchased at a price of approximately $40,000 American dollars. This home is to be used as a branch meeting place and living quarters for the missionaries. The following is a description of the property in Lima:

Mrs. Vita Vera Shoto Sanisteban is the owner of the property situated at 1210 Orrantia Avenue, corner of Los Cedros Street, in the District of San Isidro, Lima, Peru. The land area totals 675 square meters made up of one lot and a fraction of another in the Orrantia subdivision. The land was sold to the father of the above-named person, Mr. Ernest Shoto, by the Sociedad Agricola Orrantia Limitada (The Orrantia Agricultural Society Limited).

The above land total came about by joining Lot No. 390, consisting of 450 square meters and part of Lot No. 391, consisting of 225 square meters. The first mentioned lot was purchased by Mr. Ernest Shoto for his daughter, Mrs. Vita Vera Shoto Santisteban, according to the deed on the 28th of May 1936. The second parcel was purchased by Mr. Ernest Shoto for himself on the 13th of August 1940, according to the public record made by the Notary, Julio Teves. The purchaser deeded this area to his daughter on the 15th of July 1943. On this date a public document was prepared to establish the total area of 675 square meters as one property, designating the boundaries and establishing the area to be constructed.

All of the above-mentioned documents were recorded in the Public Land Registry of Lima, Peru, according to the law. The home had been a wedding gift to his daughter, but due to an accident she was not able to climb the stairs, so it was sold to the church and another one purchased. Orrantia Avenue was later changed to Jorge Bassadre.

On February 24, 1957 President Frank D. Parry presided over the first Branch Conference held in Lima, Peru. There were 33 in attendance, seven of whom were Lamanite people. The morning meeting was held in English. During the evening meeting which was held in Spanish, 44 were present, 22 of which were Peruvian investigators.

The following letter, dated March 27, 1957, was sent to the First Presidency reporting the obtaining of the *Personeria Juridica* in Peru:

> Dear Brethren: We are pleased to inform you that the Corporation of the President of the Church of Jesus Christ of Latter-day Saints is now officially recognized in Peru. The "Personeria Juridica" obtained gives us permission to practice our religion throughout the country. It further states that we can establish "sucursales" (branches) wherever we want within Peru. The Church is now officially at liberty to actuate without official restriction.
>
> We are able to obtain the "Personeria Juridica" at the right time to put the home and property purchased in Lima, Peru in the name of the Corporation of the First

Presidency. This transaction will be completed, property paid for, and deed turned over this week. We will immediately translate the deed making a plat and forward same to the legal department along with the financial breakdown and details of the purchase.

We are indebted to Brother Frederick S. Williams of Lima, Peru, for the footwork and follow through to this problem. He has been extremely helpful and cooperative in bringing this to be.

On March 31, 1958 a new Branch of the Church was organized at Ilo, Peru, with Thadeus W. Greer as President and Ingram Wilhelm Ramstrom as his counselor. Toquepala was established before 1958 by people who worked for the mine and built a chapel there. A family member, Simon Huacohar, later worked in the area office in 1985. Six hundred miles south of Lima, almost to the Chilean border, lie the three branches of Toquepala, Ilo, and Tacna. The latter two are found on your maps, whereas Toquepala, being a new settlement, is not as yet charted as a part of the geography of the "Land of the Incas". These Branches are located in the heart of a new mining area, renowned for its mineral wealth, and one of the largest mine sites in the world. About forty North American families reside in this region. A new chapel was erected in Toquepala. It overlooks the town at a height of almost nine thousand feet above sea level, making it the highest chapel of the Church in the world!

Ilo, opened for missionary work on the second day of April, 1958. Inasmuch as the North American influence was predominant, all Church meetings in Ilo as well as Toquepala, were conducted in the English language. On the other hand, in Tacna, the services were held in Spanish.

In Arequipa, the largest city of southern Peru, the missionaries commenced tracting in this picturesque spot, more or less situated 7,500 feet above sea level. Nestled in the shadows of the beautiful snow-capped volcano, "El Misti",

Arequipa is famous for year-round sunshine and exquisite flower gardens. Near the city there are ruins of an earlier civilization other than that of the Incas. October 4, 1958 was the date that the first elders arrived in Arequipa. They were Garth Taylor and Bruce Cameron.

When President Sharp was called to be the Mission President, he asked what the new mission would be called. President Henry D. Moyle said, "We don't know yet. We might call it the Peruvian-Chilean or the Chilean-Peruvian." President Sharp responded, "Well, if I might make a suggestion -- whichever name you put last, that country is going to feel slighted." After he looked again at a large map that he had on the wall and after a minute's consultation, President Moyle said, "Well, the Andes Mountains go right down through everything; let's call it the Andes Mission."

President Sharp asked him where the headquarters of the mission was to be because Santiago, Chile and Lima, Peru are as far apart as Salt Lake City and New York, and he said, "President Sharp, that will be up to you." "Well, President Moyle, what is your desire?" And he said, "I sort of prefer Santiago, Chile." President Sharp asked, "What does President David O. McKay think? What is his feeling?" "Well, he feels just as strongly that it should be Lima, Peru." "Well, I suppose that the Prophet's made the decision for us hasn't he?" President Moyle said, "Yes, it appears so."

Before dedication in Santiago, Chile, President and Sister Pace, President and Sister Lee and President Arthur Jensen proceeded with the details for the formation of the Andes Mission. In the Hotel Carrera on the mezzanine floor toward the front, they had a huge flag of Chile and a huge flag of Peru. Under the two flags with the masts crossed, a special song was written -- "Mision Andina". The words were written by Fred Williams, former president of the Argentine Mission, who was living in Lima, and it was sung by Luis Abanto

Morales, who was a favorite of the young folks, teenagers, all over Peru.

The July 18, 1959 article taken from *The Desert News* Church section read as follows: "PRESIDENT SHARP TO ORGANIZE ANDES MISSION . . . This will be President Sharp's second mission to South America, he having been one of the first missionaries to that land after it was opened for proselytizing in 1925."

On October 29, 1959 a conference was held with some 300 people in attendance (in Santiago, Chile). At this meeting Elder Harold B. Lee presented the names of the Andes Mission Presidency . . . It was explained that the southern headquarters would be in Santiago, Chile, but the main office would be in Lima, Peru . . . the Presidency and the Twelve had decided to organize a new mission to consist of the countries of Peru and Chile. The name that was chosen for this new mission was the Andes Mission. Quoting Elder Harold B. Lee, "It is proposed that we sustain as President of the Andes Mission, Brother James Vernon Sharp. . . first counselor, Joseph Robert Quayle . . . second counselor, Elder Wallace H. Baker . . . It is proposed that Sister Fawn Hansen Sharp be sustained as the President of the Relief Society and the women's' organizations of the Andes Mission . . . This is the longest mission, I guess, in the Church -- a stretch of more than 3, 000 miles of coastline and with 2,000 miles from the farthest branches to the south and the north . . . Lima, Peru, will be named the principle headquarters of the mission . . . there are seven branches with 500 members here and four branches with 300 members in Peru, or a total of eleven branches and a total of 800 members. At the present time we will have laboring in Chile 32 missionaries, and including those who will work in the office in Peru, there will be 28, or a total of 60 missionaries with which to start to work this mission."

The following are excerpts are from a stirring address given in the morning session of the Conference by Elder Harold B. Lee of the Council of the Twelve Apostles.

. . . there have been a flood of memories and thoughts running through my mind . . . where the followers of Lehi landed . . . no one knows exactly where this location was. In the wisdom of the Lord it has not been definitely revealed. We know that at the time of the crucifixion of the Lord, the whole face of the earth was changed and the arrangements of mountains and valleys and rivers may not be the same as they were before that time. But from the writings of the Prophet Joseph Smith and of other inspired men, it seems that all are in agreement that the followers of Lehi came to the western shores of South America.

There is another fact that seems clear to my mind. Where the Gospel is received by great numbers it is an evidence that there is to be found a great amount of the blood if Israel. The Prophet Joseph Smith said that. I sat here this morning thinking of what the revealed word was to Moses. In modern revelation, the Lord called Israel or those of the lineage "My chosen" and as recorded in the Bible, Moses spoke of those who came from the lineage of Jacob as the "lot of His (the Lord's) inheritance" which we have interpreted to mean the choicest of his children to come through that lineage.

It seems altogether likely that as the history of the followers of Lehi took place that there were many who didn't go with the main body as they moved northward. We know of a few groups who went out in separate groups elsewhere, some even going in ships, perhaps to the islands of the sea. The great success of the missionaries' work in some of the islands of the sea indicate that there is a great outpouring of the blood of Israel in those places.

   I have recalled today that we are now very close to the center of some of the greatest Indian populations in the world and in all likelihood, we may be near the place in these two countries of Chile and Peru where there has been a greater intermixture of Indian blood, perhaps than any other country on this continent and also the fact that there is no place in South America where there has been greater acceptance of the Gospel in so short a time.

Perhaps there are no countries where there is more advancement than in these countries on the west coast; where perhaps there is evidence of growth of stabilized government; where perhaps the economic conditions seem to be more favorable for the future and where the general living conditions are more improved than in these two countries. Here in these countries is a great outpouring of the blood of Israel. These are without question the people to whom it was said that the Gospel from the Nephite Prophets was to come.

Start studying your genealogy, get your patriarchal blessing, you will be told that you are indeed of the seed of Abraham through Isaac and Jacob and without doubt through either of the sons of Joseph -- Ephriam or Manasseh.

In the afternoon session of the conference, the organization of the Andes Mission was completed by Elder Lee:

We came this afternoon on a wonderful occasion. This marks the beginning of what appears to be a new day for missionary work in South America. It was made clear to us by President McKay, when we left Salt Lake City, that the most important purpose of our being sent was to organize the two new missions in South America. The first of those missions was organized on September 25th in Southern Brazil where the mission headquarters have been established at Curitoba, the capital city of the State of Parana. This organization today will complete what President McKay said was the most important part of our assignments. So it is about this organization and the events that have led up to it that I would like to of some events of this organization.

It was more than 108 years ago that Parley P. Pratt, a member of the Quorum of the Twelve was sent here to see if a new mission could be opened in Chile. He had been in the Pacific Islands and had now come with his wife to see the possibilities of a mission here. He landed at Valparaiso at the time of a revolution and because of the unfavorable conditions, he found it impossible to establish the mission and returned home in the following year, 1852.

Almost three-quarters of a century or seventy-four years later, or in October 1925, Elders Melvin J. Ballard, Rulon S. Wells and Rey L. Pratt were sent to Buenos Aires to dedicate the land for the preaching of the Gospel. The dedicatory prayer was offered by Brother Ballard in Palerma Park of Buenos Aires on December 25, 1925. There were some things said in that prayer which I should like you to hear:

"and now, O Father, by authority of the blessing and appointment by the President of the Church and by authority of the Holy Apostleship which I have, I turn the key, unlock and open the door for the preaching of the Gospel in those lands, and we do bless and dedicate these nations of this land for the preaching of thy Gospel."

On July 4, 1926, Elder Ballard uttered these inspired words, and as I read these words you will see a prophecy was being made that has now come to partial fulfillment. Here were some of the words which he spoke on that occasion:

"the work of the Lord will grow slowly for a time here just as an oak grows slowly from an acorn. It will not shoot up in a day as a sunflower that grows quickly and then dies. But thousands will join the Church here. It will be divided into more than one mission, and will be one of the strongest in the Church. The work here is the smallest it will ever be. The day will come when the Lamanites in this land will be given a chance. The South American Mission will be a power in the Church."

Thirty-five years after those words were uttered, five missions of the Church, approximately 10,000 members and a young army of between 400 and 500 missionaries doing work here. The work has not been sensational. It has grown slowly and steadily. Our membership has never diminished since it was established, and the greatest growth in all these missions has been in the last five years. In the Brazilian Mission for example, there were less than 1,000 members five years ago. And they now have more than 3,700 members. In 1953, 1954 and 1955, there were less than 80 members baptized into the Church in each of these years in the Argentine Mission, but last year in the Argentine Mission, there were baptized more than 600, so you see that what Brother Ballard prophesied on that occasion is now coming true.

In my judgment there are no missions in the world which hold so much promise as the missions of South America. The work is going to continue to grow, and we have not yet seen the end of the number of missions that will be established and there are those here that will see that future growth.

Likewise, the work here in Peru has been more productive in making converts than any other part of the Uruguayan mission of which this has been a part. We now have five branches in Peru: two here in the city of Lima, one at Toquepala, one at Tacna and one at Arequipa.

We now have under consideration another territory to be added to this mission . . . Bolivia. We have given consideration to this matter. It appears that at the present there are at least three excellent cities in Bolivia in which missionary work can be done. Presently it may not seem prudent to go into

Bolivia because of certain internal disturbances, but when that opportunity comes, it seems clear to us that work should be opened there. So it is therefore proposed that there be organized a new mission to be known as the Andes Mission consisting of the countries of Chile, Peru and Bolivia. (The voting was unanimous.)

It is proposed that the principal headquarters for this new mission be established at Lima, Peru. You have organized the longest mission of the Church with a coast line stretching 3,000 miles from tip to tip and the most distant branch about 2,000 miles apart.

President J. Vernon Sharp has already been named and set apart for his present calling and his wife, Sister Fawn Hansen Sharp, has likewise been called and set apart to be the president of the Relief Society and to direct the women's' auxiliaries of the new mission. The first counselor -- Brother Joseph Robert Quayle . . . his second counselor Elder Wallace Baker, one of the full-time missionaries.

Now acting for the Presidency of the Church and by the authority of my Holy Apostleship, I now declare the organization of the new Andes Mission of the Church of Jesus Christ of Latter-day Saints, the 50th mission of the Church. May the Lord bless this great mission that it may grow and flourish and this might be the beginning of even a greater effort than has ever been in the past.

A few days later, on November 5, 1959 Elder Harold B. Lee spoke to the missionaries in Lima. He said, "I have had occasions to be alone with God' . . . 'To be alone with God is one of the greatest experiences of life". Elder Lee said that men and women have had to go through many sacrifices to be proven to see if their faith is sufficiently strong. He testified that the day of sacrifice has not passed. He urged missionaries to stand by their new leaders. 'Listen to the counsel, the admonition, the instructions' . . . 'But you will find occasions when you will have to get alone with God for the answer to your problems."

It is interesting to note here that there was only one time, during his tenure, that President Sharp and his two counselors were able to meet together in the same place. The mission was a vast expanse and they did the best they could.

Chapter 6

Making Progress

It was the night before they were to visit the ruins of Macchu Pichu, President Sharp became violently ill with amoebic dysentery. An elderly doctor by the name of Perea came. This Dr. Perea would come over two or three times a day. His office was only a block from the hotel. He would come over more to chat than to see how he was getting along. The very next time that they went to the airport to process some missionaries into the country, they found that Dr. Perea was head of the Board of Health for all of Peru. He took President and Sister Sharp and introduced them to all of the customs and government officials at the airport so that they knew them all personally. Then it came time to process missionaries out of Peru and into Chile so they could work down there. He was the doctor that had to examine them physically before they could leave the country. He wouldn't charge for his services And so any time they had to have anything to do with the Board of Health in Peru, from that time on, it didn't cost them anything. There was no legal fuss, no legal muss, and also because of him, they were able to have access to go in and out of the airport where other people couldn't, to meet the Church officials and to take care of any business that they had there.

At 6:00 a.m. Saturday morning on May 18, 1960, a terrible earthquake struck. The epicenter was in Concepcion. Missionaries went right into the radio station that very day and helped with casualty lists and so on. The missionaries had a lady that cooked their meals, and they said to the young fellow at the radio station, "Will you go to a phone and call so and so and tell them we will not be home for dinner." It turned out the boy's father owned the radio station. It was on a nationwide hookup. He said, "These missionaries that are helping on these casualty lists want to get word out", so the father said, "We'll, put it on the air." And so on the air, nation-wide broadcast -- it was picked up in Argentina, and we got kidded by the missionaries over there -- "Elder so and so and Elder so and so won't be home for dinner. Please tell the maid at such and such an address not to cook them dinner."

The U.S. government was sending down two hospital units, nurses, doctors, beds, tents -- complete hospital units. They were flying them down in Globemaster planes with approximately 85 of them and nobody to translate. The missionaries went with them into the disaster areas to help.

Ten volcanoes had erupted simultaneously with the earthquake. Part of Puerto Montt and Valdivia went into the sea. In Chile, some islands sank into the ocean, some new ones came up. Missionaries were sent down with these hospital units, one by one. They did a tremendous job and were very well received by the government.

On Saturday and Sunday, December 10th and 11th, 1960, President A. Theodore Tuttle and President Joseph Fielding Smith spoke at a conference. In the afternoon session, Sister Jessie Evans Smith sang songs and talked, as well as the other Brethren who talked again.

A thing happened at the airport when they left that was the highlight of Sister Smith's trip to all of South America. One night they held a meeting in the woods out in the back. It was cold and one of the sisters brought a scarf and gave it to Sister Smith and wouldn't take it back. At the airport, when they were leaving, one of the good sisters came up with a plastic bag filled with dirt with a red, white and blue ribbon around it and she said, "Please give this to Sister Smith." President Sharp said, "Fine, thank you very much. I'll do that." And I gave it to Sister Smith and in English she said, "What is it?" And I said, "Well, to me it looks like a sack of dirt." And she said, "Ask the sister about it." So I called the sister over and I said, "Sister Smith thanks you very much. She wants to know the significance of this gift." And with pride in her voice and in her bearing she said, "That is a part of our country. I want it to link Sister Smith and me as friends and your country and our country as friends. When she goes home I would want her to plant a flower in it and when it grows and blooms that will be because of the mutual effort of our country and the United States." Now she was given many valuable gifts, -- gold brooches, and jewelry, and so on. But the thing she talked about many times on television in interviews when she returned home was that gift of a sack of dirt.

In describing the church's growth, President Sharp explained, "After consulting with President Tuttle, it was felt that we should concentrate our branches in one area so that we could have district affairs and they wouldn't feel isolated. For that reason, branches were opened were pretty much concentrated. Then they had seven steps for stakehood, to instill in the hearts of the people that ultimately we were to work to become a stake. When they opened a branch or divided a branch, they did not have to receive approval from Salt Lake to do it, but always talked it over with Brother Tuttle. If we went into a brand new area where we were starting a new branch, they found a fine house there, got a real bargain on it and leased it with an option to buy. They bought an electric range, a refrigerator, and necessary beds and necessary cooking utensils for four elders, blankets and so on. Then the elders lived in the place in which we held our meetings. That way, the elders and the Church participated in the paying of the rent. And as part of the rent, the elders paid towards the ultimate purchase of the appliances and the bedding and everything that was there. They never had a place that would accommodate less than 100 to 125 in the combination living room and dining room. We'd get a used piano and start out with 50 folding chairs."

The missionaries did not have any automobiles, but the president had one in Lima. Later, a used one was sent duty-free to Chile from Salt Lake City. The bus systems were good. Everyone went by bus or there were enough that they could hire a taxi that would go about as cheap if we all went on a bus.

Before Brother Tuttle was sent into South America, President Sharp's report was directly to the First Presidency. In starting a new mission, they were not on a budget and had very few restrictions. Instructions were given by Elder Harold B. Lee, and he gave great latitude in starting branches wherever President Sharp saw fit. Later on, of course, there was more strict supervision. President Sharp recorded, ". . . in a brand new one where everything is pretty much played by ear, you were making history, you had nothing to refer back to. It was left pretty much up to me. I know that I did receive several letters from the First Presidency complimenting me on decisions that I made, and how they felt I'd been inspired in the choice. I guess one of the biggest compliments was the letter after President Joseph Fielding Smith returned and they decided to divide the mission.

"We were supposed to have gotten missionaries at a slower pace than we did. For example, we established branches in Chile and in Peru. We had too many missionaries for the existing branches and we established new branches -- there was no language school in those days -- with a senior elder having four months, no more, in the mission. There were two places I can remember where we sent two elders and the oldest in point of service in the mission was four months. And, interestingly enough, one group baptized an entire family in the first month. They got enough newspaper publicity in the upper portion of Peru that the parent newspaper asked for an interview in Lima to find out what was going on."

President and Sister Sharp helped translate the materials for the Church during those early years. In an interview he said, "We were translating our own material. We translated the Relief Society manual in Lima, Peru. We hired a professional translator and then after the missionaries had all gone to bed at 10:30, Sister Sharp and I would go over his translation. I would translate back to English what he had written and Sister Sharp would read in English what was there and that was used for, I guess, fifteen years over the entire Church. We also translated volume one of *Growing in the Gospel* by Marie Felt. We took care of lesson preparation and translation and everything for the two organizations assigned to us."

The mission president's seminars followed pretty much the same pattern as elders' meetings in the mission in which the mission president presided. They would meet at the appointed hour of the particular day, and we would be one time in Sao Paulo, Brazil, another time in Montevideo, another time in Buenos Aires, another time in Santiago, and another time in Lima. And those in the mission where it was being held would make all of the arrangements for housing and everything else.

They would get together under the direction of President Tuttle and hold a testimony meeting. There was no limit as to time. They would talk freely of our successes and their problems and then as we had a particular success story in any one of the missions, they would go into detail later on with that and see if it worked so well in this country, why couldn't it in that country? And it was just a real workshop in which everyone took off their coats and rolled up their sleeves. They usually lasted two days. Much good came out of them. There was a bond of friendship that endures to this day. They were held two or three times a year.

The Church building program for Latin America was presented when Brother Mendenhall came down with Dyke Walton. The very first one was held in Buenos Aires, Argentina. Brother Mendenhall told the assembled group what success they had had building chapels with the help of local people in the islands and that he and the Church felt that we could do that in South America. They would send down some supervisors that would instruct basically on how the building should be built, but the actual labor would be done by the members themselves.

President Sharp recorded that Brother Mendenhall said, "Now, President Sharp, the only reason we brought you over was so you'd know the program, but your mission is too new." President Sharp took issue with that and told him that they needed it more than anybody else. As a result, he came over after the meeting. He said, "Well, I'll visit your mission and then we'll decide."

So after this mission presidents' seminar was called and they all agreed that it was a good program, that it would work and that we wanted to get it started as quickly as possible. Then he and Brother Walton came over and we met in Santiago, visited the various areas there, and talked with Brother Cifuentes and other leaders. President Sharp recorded, "We took them down to Vina del mar and showed them what we had in mind there and held meetings at Brother Mendenhall's call, so that he wouldn't figure that we had packed the meeting with folks sympathetic to us. We said, "Where do you want the meeting and at what time?" Then we'd call the meeting. He'd go in and it would be an emergency meeting. It could be Tuesday night or Wednesday night or Thursday, and just called by the elders going that day and contacting the members. We did the same thing in Peru. And he decided before he left that we'd be 100 percent in the program as were the older, established missions in South America."

In Peru they could lease buildings. In Chile, they had problems doing that, and so we bought them. The expenditure of money on the part of the Church in purchasing property and houses was double in Chile what it was in Peru.

When asked what were the procedures that they had to follow in order to purchase property President Sharp said,

"First we ascertained the need and the potential of the neighborhood. Then we got a rough estimate as to what a particular-sized piece of property would cost. Then we would write -- all of our correspondence was to the First Presidency -- and tell them that we felt the need of buying some property in Chile, whether it had a house on it or whether it didn't. We set forth in the letter the needs. Then an approximation of the amount of money that we would need and asked for their authorization to take an option on the property, if we could find it. Then the word would come back, 'Yes, go ahead.' I never once was turned down. We'd get bids and give a deposit; an option on it. Then we would write back to the First Presidency and say, 'Now, we have done this and we have done that and we have taken an option. We must know in 120 days whether we forfeit the option or whether we have your permission to proceed.' And then they would give us the permission to proceed." In just about every branch they either leased or acquired a house and property. And most of these properties were suitable for the construction of a chapel if the need arose.

There were occasional problems with visas, missionaries going from country to country, with taxes or customs or any other legal matters. Once they were having trouble with a letter that would be satisfactory to the minister of Foreign Affairs in Peru. President Sharp recorded, "We had written several and they were not acceptable, so one day the attorney's office mentioned the fact that I knew some people at Toquepala. Did I think that I could get him down so he could see the mine? I said, 'There's no problem. I can make arrangements. There will be a plane to pick you up at the airport here in Lima and take you right down there. You will be the guest of the mine at Toquepala.' We got through talking and I said, 'Now you've got me stopped. Why don't you do me a favor, now I've done you a favor? Have your secretary write a letter and phrase it the way we should phrase it so that we can get permission. Then we'll just copy it word for word onto our mission stationary.'

"He did that. And, of course, we had no problem. We were very cautious. We went through extra steps as the missionaries came in that seemed to be a lot of red tape that maybe they didn't have to do, but we did it so that there could be no problem at all. One other thing that I did, knowing that sometimes your passport might be taken if you got in any trouble with the police. I devised a card in Spanish that looked very official and had my lawyer go over it. Every missionary carried that identification besides a carnet. When I went down they just came in as tourists.

"Sister Sharp was the mission mother. Sister Sharp was also in charge of the auxiliaries in the mission; the YWMIA, the Relief Society, the Primary and things like that. Even though the mission grew and we could give responsibility, we put many folks there, but she was the top person to advise in the time that we were there. And with her experience, having been the stake president for Young Women's MIA and Relief Society president and everything else, she did a tremendous service down there. She was very well loved by the people because she diligently worked on the language and talked to them in their language rather than going through an interpreter. When she left Chile, for example, every one of the established branches of the Relief Society had a sewing machine. True, a treadle, but they had their own, and she had helped them with their projects to raise money so that each branch in Chile and in Peru when we left had their own sewing machine."

In an interview President Sharp was asked what did he feel was his greatest success? What did he enjoy most as Mission President? He responded, "The thing I enjoyed most as Mission President was the fact that Sister Sharp and I and the missionaries were not in this alone, that we had help from our Heavenly Father. In fact, Sister Sharp on many occasions said, "Why were you not this smart at home? We realized this."

"We worked diligently and long hours and hard, but we knew that if we came up against a stone wall, we had help and, confidentially, there might be a psychological reason for this; I don't know. We found after very little time in the mission that if I had a problem that was relative to my jurisdiction -- one that I had worked diligently on and couldn't find an answer -- if I prayed sincerely about it and went to bed that I would awaken at 5:00 the following morning, not with a solution, but with the idea for a solution. I also found that if I didn't write the idea down, by the time I got up at 6:00, I'd forgotten it. All I could remember was I had an idea, but I couldn't recall what it was. Sister Sharp found the same thing happening to her. Now, if it was her problem, I didn't wake up. If it was mine, she didn't wake up. If it was our problem, we both woke up and we discussed it. And so even today, we have at our bedside, a piece of paper and a pencil so we can jot down if we should get an idea. That was one thing."

The greatest difficulty or biggest problem in the mission was the health of the missionaries. President Sharp said, "That was our big worry, and we were fighting that continually. We had a lot of persecution, we had elders land in jail, but we didn't worry about that. We'd get them out . . . I didn't worry on legal affairs because on the instructions of the First Presidency, we hired the finest legal talent in the country. That was their job to take care of these legal problems. I let them worry about it. That's what they were paid for, but we did worry about the health of the missionaries. We did have arrangements in both Chile and in Peru that if an elder became ill than Lan-Chile in Chile and Faucet in Peru would even, if necessary, bump one of their passengers to take on our sick elders to get them back where we had proper medical care for them either in Santiago or in Lima."

"In Peru, we were blessed wherever we went in the things that we did. For example, we went into Trujillo to purchase property for the Church, into Chiclayo, into Arequipa. Everywhere along the line ways were opened up for us to get the exact property that we wished, at a very fair price. In the two northern cities of Chiclayo and Trujillo, we were able to get in on the ground floor with the government as they were planning new subdivisions, and before the subdivision was ever started, we had bought the property that we had wanted so we had the choice piece of property there.

In Lima, for example, they had help with the main chapel at Limatambo. "We knew ahead of time that the airport was going to be moved from Limatambo. Through our lawyer we knew the people that owned the property roundabout and before that was subdivided we knew the Pan-American Highway, where it was going to go, we knew where the shopping areas were going to go, so we bought the land there, one of the first ones before the subdivision was ever started. We felt all along that the Lord did bless us in all of our purchases there."

President Sharp commented on the final days of his mission, "We did have a tremendous Mission Presidents' seminar in June in 1962 in which all of the mission presidents in South America came over and after the seminar was over, we had in the patio of the mission home a typical Peruvian entertainment with Indian entertainers. Then we went up to Macchu Pichu and way high in the ruins of Macchu Pichu, President Theodore Tuttle rededicated all of South America again to the missionary work. It was a very inspirational time. When it came time to leave, Brother Nicolaysen was on his way down, President and Sister Tuttle came over on the day that we were to leave. We were to leave at midnight that night. We received a telephone call in the morning from Mr. Jorge Torres Lara that we talked about that helped on the Christmas program. He said, 'I don't know what you are doing at 1:00 p.m., but please be tuned into Radio Inca and have a tape recorder to record what I say.' So we got a tape recorder. We had President and Sister Tuttle and the missionaries around and at 1:00 in the afternoon he went on the air and he said, 'This is the first time in the history of Radio Inca and the first time in my history as a commentator that we have ever preempted our news program entirely and this is sponsored by the station with no charge to anybody. Some three years ago there came to our country a person representing the Church of Jesus Christ of Latter-day Saints. He brought to us a new philosophy -- his church did. His church is the only hope that we have for the Peruvian Indians. His church, through the Word of Wisdom, is the only hope that we have to break the habit of chewing the coca leaf that the Indian people have. I didn't feel it fitting that this man should leave without his church and him knowing how we appreciate what they have done for our country.'

"Then he had a recording that he played from the Tabernacle Choir, and he went on and he told of the things that had been done, how in his particular case, when he had a child that was ill, the doctors had been too busy to come, but that he called the elders and called me, and we went right over and administered to his child and his child was healed. And he, for half an hour, told of all of these things that the Church had done and what we could expect from the Church. He was at the airport, of course, to see us off even though it was midnight. He was very high in his praise of the Church, in the hope that it offered for all of the people of Peru. But we gave a copy to Church Information and to the Spanish Language Department, and they rebroadcast it many times over their international program in Spanish.

About 2:00 in the afternoon we received a call that two of our missionaries had been put in jail because of that program. So I called the archbishop of Lima. He had been made a cardinal, and I had met him a couple of times in various airports and had chatted with him. So as I talked to him I told him I had called him up to tell him good-bye, but also that maybe I couldn't leave that midnight. He wondered why. And I said, "Well, a couple of your eager Franciscan friars have pressed charges against our elders for a radio program that was on Radio Inca." I said, "Did you hear that program?", and he said, "Yes, I want to congratulate you on the fine work you have done down here and how much those folks respect and admire you, and respect and admire your church." And I said, "Well, you know, they don't belong to our Church, they belong to your church. Now it was spontaneous, we knew nothing about it until I got a telephone call telling us to tune in on it. Now I can't leave with my missionaries in jail. You can understand why. And I don't want to go to the press or the radio and tell them why I couldn't leave. Your relations and mine have been too good to do that." He said, "I don't know anything about it." And I said, "Of course you don't, but you can take care of it." So within half an hour, they were out of jail. So that was the last day in the mission field. So you can see the Lord was helping us right up to the very end.

President Sharp ordained some brethren to the priesthood, "but we didn't tell the people that we had that program, because we didn't want to build up their hopes. One thing I did not want to do, which is so often done in Latin America, is to promise things and not deliver. I would sooner not promise and then by surprise deliver than to have them expect something."

"I was elated with the progress that we were making and with the type of individuals. Now we didn't go after the extreme upper class, nor did we go after the extreme lower class. The missionaries under my direction, since we were having to develop leaders to take positions, worked -- and it was a slow process -- with the upper middle class -- doctors, lawyers, merchants, nurses and so on -- people that we could give responsibility to. Now we realized that it would take a little longer to convert them than perhaps if we went down to a little lower strata of education and so on. But we were frantic. As the mission was growing, we were having to get leadership. I had had experience in Mexico and had seen where the missionaries had been taken out and put back, and taken out and how things had fallen away when the missionaries were taken out. And so I suspect that I was more keenly aware of this than other people would have been, and so we specifically zeroed in on ones who could be leaders.

At first, the missionaries played a big role in directing the branches. As they first went in, it was 100 percent missionaries. And then, as the branch developed and we had the leadership, then they would go pretty much into an advisory capacity. Then, as the members began to see the format, we shifted from missionaries to the native branch presidents, or the native district presidents so that they could take charge. But it was a slow educational process and, of course, many things came up unexpectedly because you give a directive and it isn't always interpreted the way you think it's going to be. You have to be prepared for that and not get angry, because they're doing the best they can."

There were twenty missionaries in at the beginning of the Andes Mission. As of September 1961, when the mission was divided, there was sixty-five in Peru, plus four in the office to supervise the others. On November 1, 1959, there were four branches in Peru. As of September 27, 1961, there were twelve branches in Peru. On November 1, 1959, there were less than 800 members in the Andes Mission, on September 27, 1961, there were 2,000 members in the Andes Mission, so we had grown by 1,200 in two years. November 1, 1959, there was one district in Peru. September 27, 1961, there were two districts in Peru. November 1, 1959, we owned two houses in Peru. September 27, 1961, we owned two houses and two lots in Lima and had money appropriated to buy a lot in Arequipa. In Toquepala, Peru we owned one chapel.

President Sharp explained that "The Mission Presidents have sources of information in the areas in which they live that the missionaries don't have. When President Prado was overthrown, we knew at least ten days before he was ousted as president that it was going to happen. It was a bloodless affair. He went to a big reception and was the guest of honor at the reception. About 1:00 a.m. in the morning, he went to the presidential palace; about 2:00 a.m. in the morning, tanks surrounded the presidential palace and gave him two minutes to come out. Of course, he couldn't get out in two minutes, and so they broke down one of the outer gates, went in with the tank, loaded him in an automobile, took him out to Callao, put him on a warship, sailed him around out in the bay around Callao for a couple or three days and finally decided that he was to go into exile to France. His wife was of French descent. In the eulogy to him they said he was the best president they had ever had, but still they had ousted him. And it was a bloodless affair. Perhaps he even helped choose his successor.

"Many of the upper families, the ruling families in politics in Latin America are intermarried; because upper class is a small percentage. So if from this sort of a royal family, as it were, they take out one, the one they put in might be his cousin or his uncle or something like that. And so we had no problem; our contacts that we had made remained the same. Now we were careful and told our missionaries always of an experience that I had. And that they, if anybody wanted to talk politics, that they were to say: "We know nothing of the politics of your country. We do know about the Gospel; let's talk about it."

"And I told them a thing that happened to me once in Mexico during the Revolution. I had a man put a gun in my back. I didn't know who he was, and he said, "Quien vive?" (Who are you for?) and I thought quickly, and I said, "Yo vivo." (For myself.) "Yo vivo", and he laughed. Then he said, "Boy, you said the right thing." And I never did find out which side he was on. And so that was our instruction to our missionaries, that the Church takes no part in any politics at all in the country. We support whoever is there and any change they make. That is their business. We support them 100 percent.

"We were trying to create a good feeling between not only the missionaries in the two countries, but the members of the Church in the two countries to let them know that the Gospel is worldwide and that we don't let petty things worry us. But I found out after a year that this didn't work too well because the very missionaries that we would send to Chile for the first year or year and a half and bring them up to Peru, had built up an antipathy towards the Peruvians. The elders themselves would get into some discussions. So we dropped that idea after about a year, a year and a half. We'd divide them, bring them and process them into Lima and then get them immediately into Chile, and then we wouldn't do the interchanging. Our first theory was to have them work half their mission in one country and half in the other, but it didn't work out."

"Regarding publications, a weekly newsletter called the *Chasqui* (the Messenger) went out each week from the mission office. There were occasional problems with negative publicity from the local papers or on television. We'd go in and open a new area, and I thought that many of the Catholic folks who directed their propaganda against the Church weren't too intelligent. I had this happen in Argentina first. There was a big article when Brother Ballard and President Pratt were there about the Mormons were down and the elders were looking for wives. Well, after that article in the paper, we had a dozen people come to Church to see us, to see what kind of guys were looking for wives and some of our converts were of that group. And so we found that adverse publicity helped us because as they went on and on, they were so far out that a thinking person would know that it couldn't be true.

"Let me tell you a specific incident that happened on the border between Peru and Chile -- it actually happened in Tacna, Peru. We had some elders there and two Catholic priests from North America, Marinol fathers, came down and after a while they began to say all manner of things against the missionaries, among other things, that they were homosexual.

And the head of the Catholic youth organization said, 'That can't be. I play basketball with those guys on Monday, that's their free day. They aren't that kind of guy.'

And they had a bunch of other lies about them. And so he did some investigating. Within a month, the Catholic people drove those two Marinol fathers out because they found that they were homosexuals and this head of the Catholic youth group joined the Church and later became the branch president. So we found that if we didn't get into a fight, we didn't get into a debate, we just stated our case and what we were there for; that every time they went into a program against us and every time we went into a new area, the Catholic people did zero in on us on radio and television and newspapers, but it was to our advantage every time. All we asked of the missionaries was that they conduct themselves as missionaries."

Chapter 7

Making History

Enrique Ruis Ortega was the first person to be baptized in Ica, one of the major cities south of Lima. He was baptized August 30, 1960 by Elder Deli. Sometime later his wife, Antoneate Teresa Ditolidi Gonzales, was baptized, September 15, 1960 along with her children, Cesar and Maria.

In November, Elder Ezra Taft Benson visited Lima as emissary for the U.S. government. December 18, 1960: Conference was held in Lima. The presiding authority was President Joseph Fielding Smith who came with his wife, Jesse Evans Smith the accomplished singer. On Christmas day President and Sister Sharp took President and Sister Smith to a meeting in each of the branches in Lima. The spirit of Christmas was everywhere. Each branch was honored by the presence of an Apostle of the Lord. The New year began with a tour of the mission. President Sharp recorded the following humorous account:

> During the tour of the Andes Mission, the Smiths, Sister Sharp and myself had projected a tour to Southern Peru. We arose early and at 5:00 a.m. as we were leaving the mission home, Sister Smith handed Sister Sharp one of her dresses and said, "Will you put a note on this dress and have it sent to the cleaners while we are away?" Sister Sharp did this. When we returned after several days, we were met by Flora, our housekeeper, who was in tears. She could neither read nor write in any language. She was the first to see the dress and proceeded to wash it and it shrunk to about twenty inches long and one foot wide. Sister Smith said, "What do we do?" Sister Sharp answered, "In the city of Lima, we will never find another. Let's do this. Let's dampen the dress over again, put it on the ironing

board, and I will press it while President Smith pulls on one end and you pull on the other." They did this and it turned out beautifully. In fact, at a later General Conference in Salt Lake City, Sister Smith came up to Sister Sharp and said, "Look, I am still wearing our dress." (Letter to Dale Christensen dated December 16, 1985)

On October 1, 1961, a District Conference was held with all the missionaries in Peru in attendance. In the morning session of Conference there were 441 in attendance. President A. Theodore Tuttle, the visiting Authority, recommended the division of the Andes Mission because of the growth in two years and the great distance involved. He gave the boundaries of the two missions and the names. The Andes Mission to include Peru, Bolivia and the city of Arica in Chile because of it being so near Tacna in Peru. The new Chilean Mission to include all of Chile with the exception of the city of Arica. With Delbert Palmer as President of the new Chilean Mission.

The Northern Peruvian District was divided on November 18, 1961 to form the Central Peruvian District. The branches in this new District will be Mariategui, San Isidro, Balconcillo, Miraflores and Cuzco; that was opened this same day.

May 14, 1962: A new branch was opened in the city of Huacho with Elder John L. Blake as Branch President. The branch was officially opened June 17th.

May 20, 1962: The first meeting in the new Barranco Branch was held. There were twenty-five in attendance. Leonard Ki Shield was named Branch President.

April 23, 1962: In the Branch of La Florida, the testimonies of members and elders were strengthened by the healing of Sister Fortunado de Manco of an illness suffered for over a year after being anointed and blessed by Elders J. Bingham, H. Martinez and G. Romney. Through her faith and the power and blessing of the Lord, Sister Manco was completely cured of a chronic allergic condition.

May 24, 1962: The North Peru District was divided into two districts, the new one being named North Central Peru, with Elder Douglas S. Rose as President and Elder Terry Korous as his Assistants.

May 30, 1962: President and Sister Sharp, President Tuttle and the supervising elders, Jay Payne and Donald Jones drove to Mollendo, Peru. There President Sharp signed the contract for a house in which to begin a new branch, thus fulfilling a prophecy made by Apostle Melvin J. Ballard and Rey L. Pratt as they visited that city in June of 1926, saying that missionaries would someday bring the Church of Jesus Christ of Latter-day Saints to the city of Mollendo, Peru.

June 23, 1962: Three elders went to Ica to open a branch there. They were Elders Kay B. Cleverly, John D.A. Neil and Brian J. Greer. On the same day, President and Sister Sharp and President and Sister Tuttle arrived to see the branch.

June 26, 1962: In President Tuttle's prayer, he rededicated this land to the work of the Lord.

July 1, 1962: The first Sacrament Meeting of the Mollendo Branch was held between the elders. On July 15, the Mollendo Branch held its first Sacrament Meeting open to the public.

July 2, 1962: President and Sister Sharp today received an honorable release from the Andes Mission. The new President will be Sterling Nicolaysen.

July 7, 1962: The Huacho Branch had its first baptismal service with four missionaries and one member present.

July 7, 1962: President Sharp divided the North-Central and Central-Andean Districts. The new district is the South Central Andean District and will be presided over by President Kay B. Cleverly. The branches in the Northern Central Andean District are: Callao, Magdalena, Pueblo Libre and Huacho.

July 22, 1962: President Sharp ordained Gidalthi Ojeda as Priest, the only member in Cuzco.

August 5, 1962: The first Branch Meeting was held in Piura today with 35 persons in attendance.

August 18, 1962: The first baptismal service in Cuzco was held in the River Vilcanota, about 40 kilometers from Cuzco. There were 25 in attendance to witness the baptism.

August 20, 1962: President and Sister James Vernon Sharp left Peru for the USA, completing their service as President of the Andes Mission. They were released today and left August 21st.

August 29, 1962: The Capital District was formed which includes the branches of San Isidro, Pueblo Libre and Balconcillo.

January 6, 1963: The Sur-Andino District was formed with Marion Carl Robinson (father) as President includes the three branches in Arica, Chile; Tacna and Toquepala, Peru.

February 9, 1963: President Hugh B. Brown, President and Sister Tuttle and President and Sister Nicolaysen met with the four Cuzco Elders. President Brown spoke of his concern for the future of the work in Cuzco. He gave inspired counsel about the enduring spirits of the ancient Book of Mormon Prophets who will labor with us to see that the work of the Restored Church develops in Cuzco. He spoke of the leadership yet to come from among these Lamanite people and referred to the possibility of a great leader -- even an apostle of the Lord -- being called in the future (perhaps as long hence as fifty years) from among the converts of elders now laboring in this area. President Tuttle dismissed the meeting with prayer and a blessing, referring to the strength the elders would need to convert those who would be able to go out as Quecchua-speaking missionaries to reach the chosen people who populate the mountain regions. This was a meeting of hope and reassurance.

Soon after Elder Joseph Groberg, as a new missionary, arrived in the Andes Mission, he wrote home, "President Hugh B. Brown spoke to us. While in Cuzco, a dark feeling had come over him. He was going to suggest to the Mission President that the Elders be taken out of that area. Then, in the meeting with the Elders, he felt the presence of another person whose spirit influenced him. It was Samuel the Lamanite." (Elder Boyd K. Packer mentioned similar impressions at the dedication of the Lima Temple site.)

February 10, 1963: Conference day in Lima with President Hugh B. Brown and President and Sister A. Theodore Tuttle. The morning and afternoon sessions were held in the Cine Ambassadore. Excursion groups from many branches attended, including members from Huacho and Trujillo. Attendance in the morning session was 1009, and in the afternoon session, 891. After each of the conference sessions, baptismal services were held with a total of 18 persons being baptized as a result of the conference. Considerable favorable attention was received from the press in preparation for the conference and President Brown's visit, and special attention was given by the press to the participation of the district choir -- El Coro Polifonico Mormon.

March 8, 1963: There was a march against the Church. The following account was written by President Luis Montalvan: "At 8:00 p.m. Friday, a Catholic demonstration occurred in front of the branch. It was headed by the parish of the Catholic Church, La Immaculado (Azangaro). In this demonstration, they brought an image of the crucified Christ. The demonstration was characterized by the hostility shown, and the insults spoken reaching the point of painting the walls of the branch with insults. The demonstration lasted 30 minutes. At the end of the demonstration, there were a few conflicts brought about by sympathizers to the Church who tried to block the demonstration with reproaches toward the Catholic priest who directed the demonstration. When the demonstration ended, many friendly people came to express their indignation towards these Catholics.

April 17, 1963: Three missionaries arrived this morning from the United States: Elder Duane Bryon Chase and Elder and Sister Edmund Fehr. Brother and Sister Fehr are the first married couple to do missionary work in the Andes Mission.

Chapter 8

Hope Through Adversity

The case of Elder Phillip Terry Styler who is lost in the Machu Picchu area was recorded on May 29, 1963. President Nicolaysen and Elder Randall Huff departed from the hotel at 6:00 a.m. with the judge from Urabamba, his scribe and two members of the Guardia Civil to inspect the sites on Huayna Picchu (the peak adjacent to the ruins of Machu Picchu) which figure in the case of Elder Styler's disappearance. The scribe left the group soon because of mountain climbing difficulties. The ascent to the top of the peak, the Temple of the Moon, on the far side of the peak about mid-way down its slope, and the return to the hotel were completed in about four hours. The judge completed the writing of his observations in the hotel and granted provision of certificates to the effect that Elder Styler was lost and presumed the victim of a fatal accident; also, that Elder Reese Randall Huff, his companion, was free of any responsibility for the accident according to the evidence then available.

The following is a summary of the case of Elder Phillip Terry Styler and his unfortunate disappearance while visiting the ruins of Machu Picchu en-route home from his mission in Uruguay. First, a simple review of the happenings on the day of Elder Styler's disappearance. On May 16, the two elders, Elder Styler and his companion, Elder Reese Randall Huff, left the tourist hotel at the ruins of Machu Picchu and hiked to the top of the peak which is called Huayna Picchu. On the top of the peak they stopped to take some photos. Elder Huff remained there in order to rest and take more pictures while Elder Styler went down the ridge a short distance to take other pictures and look at the landscape. He called to Elder Huff asking that Elder Huff go down to see the view from that point, but Elder Huff did not immediately follow him.

After about 15 minutes, Elder Huff realized that he could not see his companion and he called to him loudly. There was no reply, and then he began to follow his companion's tracks down the trail that he seemed to have followed toward a ruin called The Temple of the Moon. As he descended, he kept calling repeatedly, and one time he heard an answer. He knew that it was his companion's voice, but he could not understand the few words spoken. There was nothing in the manner in which is companion answered at that time to make Elder Huff feel that Elder Styler was in distress; rather Elder Huff believes that only the density of the growth and the roar of the river below as well as the distance which separated them after about 15 or 20 minutes made it difficult to understand the response.

Finally, having seen various indications in the dirt that his companion had followed the same trail, Elder Huff arrived at The Temple of the Moon. There he did not realize that it was possible to go further down a trail toward the river. He thought that the beginning of such a trail was a dead end into a ruined wall and turned instead along a more noticeable trail which led back around the peak and rejoined the trail which went through the ruins and to the hotel itself.

Elder Huff sincerely believed that Elder Styler was probably ahead of him on the trail and that he would meet his companion in the hotel. Such was not the case, and Elder Huff so advised the hotel manager and employees of his companion's disappearance. There was an exhaustive search for several days using missionaries, military and archeological personnel.

In conclusion, President Nicolaysen wrote, "After this on-the-spot observation, I am convinced that Elder Huff's theory about his companion's disappearance is probably correct. Prior to their separation at the top of the peak, Elder

Huff said that his companion had asked about the possibility of seeing what was on the other side of the mountain. Elder Huff says that he had responded to the effect that any descent to that side would be pointless, since they would only have to finally encounter the river and return by a laborious hike upstream to the point where the hotel buses cross from the railroad over the river bridge on a long, dusty, curving ascent up the side of the mountain to the tourist hotel. Elder Huff believes that the possibility of doing this was in his companion's mind."

When Elder Styler reached the point slightly below The Temple of the Moon where he must have made his decision to continue on down the trail, we can see that his first observations would make him think that the river was close and the descent relatively easy. Actually, that is not the case, and he must have found it almost impossible to even consider returning back up the trail he took; yet it is not likely that he was much disturbed, since he had considered a return to the river bridge along the river bank feasible. The tracks which were discovered on Tuesday lead upstream to a point where passage on the river bank itself is impossible. A sheer cliff rises on the right, the river is on the left, and a very large rock obstructed his travel.

There is no indication in the tracks which were found that Elder Styler was alarmed. Those who observed the fresh tracks report that no tracks return back in the direction from which the Elder would have come, nor was there any sign of his having milled around in indecision. He left no clothing on the bank, nor did he deposit his camera there. We, therefore, believe that his decision about how he would get around the rock was not one of desperation or alarm. It is assumed that he probably tried to pass in the water close to the rock; however, tests indicate that the water was not shallow there, nor is the stream slow at that point. It makes a very rapid descent, and when the accident occurred, there was a heavy flow and a strong current.

It is almost out of the question that a person slipping from the top of the rock or stepping into the water alongside the rock and caught in the current would have been able to survive for a very long distance. The stream is cascading and falling rapidly at this point, and it is feared that a person would be badly battered in a short distance. Points downstream from Machu Picchu were alerted to watch for the Elder or for any floating objects in the river. Native people in the surrounding area have been offered some reward if they could locate the Elder. There have been no reports to this date.

In addition to the problems of conducting a proper search and determining how long it should continue, we have been involved in the separate matter of seeing that Elder Huff properly complied with the requests of local authorities to furnish information about the accident and to submit to their investigation of the case.

<u>June 18, 1963</u>: President Sterling Nicolaysen, President David Smith and the Branch Presidency visited Brother Nolberto Gonzales Cornejo in the Hospital de las Mercedes. Brother Gonzales received severe burns while working in his bakery. The burns covered his entire body. On June 18th, Brother Gonzales asked that he be given a blessing by President Nicolaysen. The blessing was given by President Edmundo Carrion of the Chiclayo Branch. The doctors stated that Brother Gonzales would have to remain in the hospital for at least three months for treatments and that he would be scarred. Immediately after the blessing, Brother Gonzales healed rapidly; so rapidly that the doctors considered it a "miracle". On June 30th, Brother Gonzales attended the Sunday School service and was in good health. He left the hospital practically unscarred after receiving treatment for only ten days, expressed a sincere desire to become a missionary on the construction program and prepared himself for his call which he began on August 15th 1963 at the Magdalena project.

September 8, 1963: President Nicolaysen interviewed President Carlos Rodriguez and his wife, Sister Lily Rodriguez and issued them temple recommends to be used in the Arizona Temple where they will be sealed to each other and to their children during the "Lamanite" temple session soon to be conducted in the Arizona Temple. President and Sister Rodriguez are the first convert couple from the Andes Mission to receive recommends to attend a temple for their own endowments and sealing.

September 12, 1963: Sister Ruth Ojeda was the first convert to fill a full-time mission in the Andes Mission. She was interviewed today prior to her honorable release and returned to her home in Arequipa.

September 18, 1963: The first group of elders who had been trained in the new Language Institute at Brigham Young University for the Andes Mission arrived in Lima and began their orientation in the mission home.

September 30, 1963: Sister Maria Van German was baptized at Cochabamba, Bolivia, in a private swimming pool. The ordinance was performed by Edward Hansen, a priest. Although there are a few members of the Church who live in Bolivia, either North Americans on special assignment or citizens who have been baptized while they were out of Bolivia in other missions, this baptism was to the President, the first baptism and confirmation performed in Bolivia in these latter days.

December 27, 1963: Notification was received by cable from Sister Alwina Hulme, member of the Church in La Paz, Bolivia, that the government had issued its formal decree granting the request of the Church for registration of the corporation of the Presiding Bishopric in Bolivia. This information was relayed to President Tuttle in Montevideo and to the Office of the First Presidency. Final baptismal reports for the year 1963 were prepared showing a total number of 1,566 convert baptisms for the year.

February 2, 1964: President Tuttle's tour had aroused considerable interest among the leading Catholic clergymen in Tacna and Arequipa, and the Bishop in Tacna had issued a special order to local Catholics, forbidding them to attend any sessions conducted by President Tuttle, indicating to them that any participation by Catholics in Mormon meetings would subject them to excommunication. This same approach was taken by the Archbishop of Arequipa, and the Pastoral orders were publicized repeatedly in local newspapers. The following articles were published in Arequipa giving an example of such publications:

WARNING TO CATHOLICS: Don't join with Mormons!

Catholics: If you don't wish to be excommunicated, refrain from any direct contact whatsoever with those belonging to the Mormon Sect warned Archbishop's Palace yesterday.

The Archbishop's statement was provoked by the arrival of national Mormon leader Theodore Tuttle, who is currently inspecting but they do exhibit a very distinct point of view.

The Archbishop's Palace, upon learning of the case, declared that excommunication is the punishment for Catholics who affiliate with the Mormon Church.

Attendance of Catholics at any social or public events directed by the Mormons is also sanctioned with lesser penalties.

The Church's statements have come in conjunction with the presence of Tuttle. In Tacna, the

Bishop has published warnings to its members against the Mormons.

May 1964:CAUTION WITH THE MORMONS!!! Attention, Catholics, Attention!

The insidious, anti-evangelistic Mormon propaganda in the form of eye-catching literature had reached our peaceful town of Arequipa, which has always been so associated with Catholicism that it can be affirmed that which is not Catholic is not Arequipan.

Be careful, Catholics: a great moral danger threatens you. Mormon propaganda is highly crafty and deceiving. It speaks to you of God, of Christ, of the Gospel . . . and that would seem sufficient to you, you may even come to believe it is the same as Catholicism without realizing that it speaks nothing of submission to the Church, of receiving its sacraments, etc.; even though this is clearly part of the Holy Gospel. Moreover, the Mormon propaganda wants to take you to the edge of Gospel truth, to keep you from the Life of Grace. It simply wants to deceive you.

Be careful, Catholics. Don't be taken by the Yankee Mormons, who, with their ingenuousness you see earning large amounts of dollars for every Catholic they can trap with their nets; so that the small gifts they will give you result very fruitful for them economically.

February 6, 1964: Sister Lily Rodriguez was called to be the first local member President for the Mission Relief Society Board.

June 9, 1964: President and Sister A. Theodore Tuttle spoke at a special meeting which emphasized different manners of activating more members, efficiency in the work, the support needed from wives of church leaders, and strict adherence to standards. The following article appeared in the newspaper "El Sol" in Cuzco on June 9, 1964:

MORMON LEADER COMES TO PERU

In making an extensive tour of South American countries, Elder Spencer W. Kimball, one of the twelve Apostles of the Church of Jesus Christ of Latter-Day Saints (Mormon) is overlooking development of the Church in our country. Currently he is in charge of the Missionary Department of the Church, particularly among the native people of North and South America. The Mormon Church's program for these people is a complete plan of development. The Church runs a series of schools, Institutes of Religion, etc. to aid in the growth of these people.

The Church of Jesus Christ of Latter-Day Saints, commonly known as the Mormon Church, has great interest in the Indian people of North and South America. This interest is based upon the belief that these people, inhabitants of America, were visited by Jesus Christ and taught the Gospel. Therefore, the Mormon Church now operates a large plan of development for them. It consists in establishing institutes for the teaching and education of the many, many Indian descendants. In more than 200 schools in the United States there are special classes for them.

Currently there are 280 missionaries dedicating full time to the teaching of the Indians.
The Church has established a committee to study the conditions of the Indians and aid in their progress. The Committee President, Elder Spencer W. Kimball, one of the twelve Apostles of the Church, is visiting Peru. He will tour several sites during his time here to oversee and study the growth of the Church in Peru. He will direct a press conference during his time in Peru.

June 12, 1964: Elder and Sister Kimball and party returned from La Paz to Lima and went directly to the national Palace of Peru where Elder Kimball, President Tuttle and President Nicolaysen had an interview with President Belaunde Terry, the President of Peru. President Belaunde's concern for conditions in the more remote areas of Peru, the Andean region and the Amazon basin area, was very noticeable, and he indicated some concern over the fact that the Church's expansion in Peru was still limited to coastal centers of relatively high population. The general spirit of the interview was cordial, and the President accepted some literature related to the Church.

June 20, 1964: President Nicolaysen, President Groberg and Elder Franklin Fenlon traveled to Arequipa to participate in Arequipa District Conference. At 3:30 p.m. a groundbreaking ceremony was held in Arequipa chapel site. Excellent arrangements had been made, and the U.S. Consul and the Alcarede for Yanahuara were presented at the ceremony.

August 16, 1964: The North Andino District was officially organized in a special conference session held in Chiclayo with 350 members of the Pirua, Chiclayo and Trujillo Branches in attendance. President Edmundo Carrion was sustained without counselors.

August 27, 1964: President Nicolaysen received instructions from President Theodore Tuttle giving permission to inaugurate the work in Bolivia.

October 11, 1964: The following story tells of a marvelous healing by the Hand of the Lord:

> I was dying. The Lord told me that He was going to try my faith because I had a doubt. I did not believe in the Celestial Kingdom. He asked me if I believed it now and I told Him, "Yes, Lord." "I am going to take you there."

"No, Lord, don't take me." "Now I am going to take you with Me." "No, Lord, I don't want to die."

Brother Brown explained to her that he had heard her say those things, but that he had not heard the other side of the conversation. He also told her that there was yet more to the experience that she had not told, and she nodded to the affirmative. He then told her again that these things were sacred and for her to repeat them only to those who had a lot of faith. He asked her if they should stop at the Tacna Hospital rather than go to Arica which was one hour further away. She said, "El Senor, me ha sanado ya." (Translated means The Lord has already healed me.) This indicated she did not need the services of a hospital . . . This is part of the account written up by Brother Marvin Brown and signed by him.

November 7, 1964: President A. Theodore Tuttle and Elder Boyd Packer arrived in Lima and made arrangements to travel to Cuzco the following day where they participated in special meetings with the missionary elders and conducted an unusually inspiring Branch Sacrament meeting. A description of this experience was recorded many years later in an address given by Elder Boyd K. Parker at the dedication of the Brazil Temple in November 1978. This following account was also included on pages 134-136 in Elder Packers book *That All May Be Edified* in a chapter entitled "We Are Going to Find Him":

My dear brothers and sisters, it is a great privilege to present a message in this historic and sacred meeting for the temple dedication. I hope we will be united by the Spirit at this time.

When I am in South America there is someone I always look for. I first met him fourteen years ago in Cuzco, Peru, the ancient city in the top of the Andes.

Brother Tuttle and I were attending a sacrament meeting in the Cuzco Branch. We were seated at one end of the room facing the congregation. Behind the congregation was a door which opened onto the street. Against the wall to our left was a small sacrament table. The room was full of people. The door to the street was open for the cool night air to enter.

(The Boy) While Brother Tuttle was speaking, a little boy appeared in the doorway. He was perhaps six or seven years old. His only clothing was a tattered shirt which almost reached his knees. He was dirty and undernourished, with all the characteristics of a street orphan. Perhaps he entered the room to get warm, but then he saw the bread on the sacrament table.

He began to approach, carefully walking next to the wall. When he was just about to reach the sacrament table, one of the sisters saw him. Without saying a word, with only a movement of her head, she clearly communicated the message, "out". He hesitated an instant, turned around, and disappeared into the night. My heart wept for him. Undoubtedly the sister felt justified because this was a special meeting, with General Authorities present, and this was a dirty little boy who wasn't going to learn anything, and after all, he wasn't even a member of the Church.

In a short time he appeared in the doorway again, looking toward the bread. Again he began to quietly approach the table. He had almost reached the row where the woman was sitting when I got him to look at me. I held out my open arms. He came to me, and I picked him up to hold him in my arms.

(They Are Ours) I felt that I had an entire people in my arms. It was a deeply moving experience. Dirty little boys and girls, in tatters, are not offensive to me, nor are their brave parents repugnant to me because they are ours.

In order to teach the members an important principle, I had the child sit in President Tuttle's seat. When the meeting ended, he got down from the seat and darted out into the night. I have looked for him since then.

Now he would be old enough to serve a mission, so I have looked for him in missionary meetings in Chile, Peru, Ecuador, Colombia, and Brazil. Perhaps he is married now with his own child in tatters. I have hoped to see him in some conference or leadership meeting. I have looked for his face in the congregations. Many times I have thought I saw him in a crowd of people, or beside the road, or in the Indian market. He would be taller now, and would no longer appear in our doorway on his own. It must be harder now to enter. He was innocent then -- but now?

Perhaps he has a sister. I have also looked everywhere for her. I have looked in our meetings among the sister missionaries -- everywhere. Some must think it is a search in vain, but we are going to find them, because we are going to check all the souls in South America.

Perhaps we won't find him until his own children have grown in stature or have their own children, but we are going to find him. Perhaps someone may say that he has died, that he has gone away. We will find him anyway. We will sort through all the names, every soul who has lived in South America, to make sure we haven't overlooked him.

(A Voice from the Dust) I felt something when I held that child in my arms. A voice from the dust, perhaps from the dust of those small feet, already rough, whispered to me that this was a child of the covenant, of the lineage of the prophets. When we find him, and we are going to find him, we will bring him here to the temple -- clean, well nourished, and pure -- to be endowed and to kneel for sacred sealings. If he has departed, his son will come here in his place.

I have been in Cuzco since that time, and now I see this people whom I held in my arms, coming to be baptized, to preach, to preside. They will find him. Some day perhaps he will be there in Cuzco in a sacrament meeting as one of the twelve chosen Apostles. He will bear witness as I bear witness, that the day of the children of Laman and Lemuel and Nephi has come, that the Book of Mormon, the voice from the dust, is true. He will bear witness as I bear special witness that Jesus is the Christ, the Son of God, the Only Begotten of the Father. In the name of Jesus Christ, Amen.

August 13, 1965: President Arvil Jesperson and family, including his wife, Doris, and children, arrived in the Andes Mission.

October 8, 1965: Today the land of Ecuador was dedicated and opened for proselytizing. Quito, Ecuador (Friday) -- Exert from the Dedicatory Prayer by Elder Spencer W. Kimball:

Father, in this land called Zion, in a place known to Thee , Thy Beloved Son didst come to the ancestors of these people and didst teach them the restored Gospel those centuries are from which great truth here has been a great apostasy and the truths of Thine everlasting Gospel were lost to all the world as well as to these chosen people, but through Thy grace and goodness, it has been restored to the world, but has not yet been relayed back to this people.

Our Father, we remember Thy son, Lehi, prayed, oh, how he prayed for his descendants and prophesied that they would not be utterly destroyed so that they might receive the truths of the Gospel, we remember that Thy son, Nephi, didst continually cry unto Thee through the days and wet his pillow with tears by night as he contemplated in prophetic vision the great tribulations to which his people would be subjected, and he wept for them.

Father, we remember Thy son, Enos, after he had received a remission of his own sins, he began to pray with his whole soul for his own brethren, the Nephites, and Thou didst promise him that the Nephites would be given every blessing which they merited by their service and righteous living. And when he did cry in mighty prayer unto Thee with great fervor, and with faith undaunted, that Thou wouldst remember the Lamanites, and Thou didst promise to him that Thou wouldst bring the truth unto the Lamanites, that they would not perish with the Nephites, and this according to the faith of Thy son, Enos.

Oh, Father, Thou dost remember Thy Lamanite son and prophet, Samuel, and the numerous ones between Lehi and Moroni, who wept and prayed and fasted and struggled for their people, that they might not be destroyed, that they might have the opportunities of life and eternity. Now, our Father, they have been scattered according to Thy prophecies -- scattered from the ends and the width of this great American world. Now, we pray, our Father, that we may have reached the time when the Lamanites may hear the Gospel and join the true church and be gathered in every deed. Holy Father, we ask, have they not waited long enough through these interminable centuries? Have they not suffered enough in pain, anguish, deprivation, ignorance? Have these centuries not been long enough?

Father, bless, we pray Thee, all the people, that they may open their hearts. We ask Thee to frustrate the designs of the evil one who will do all in his power to destroy this work. Father, change and soften the hearts of the leaders of other churches who made strenuous efforts to destroy the work almost before it is born. Bless these Indian folks, that they may accept the truths; for Thy Gospel will bring to them numerous blessings: shoes upon their feet, clothes upon their backs, houses in which to live, church in which to worship Thee and communication and transportation and all the luxuries and lovely things which are Thine to give.

Our Father, Thou hast promised us that when Thy people live the commandments that Thou wilt prosper them. The ancestors of these folks have been prospered numerous times and then, through wickedness, have lost all that they had gained through prosperity. Bless them now, we pray, Heavenly Father. Our hearts are shedding tears this night, begging and imploring Thee to take care of the elements for the good of this cause. Raise up friends to the Church and its people. Take care of all political business and industrial situations so that the chains and feeters that have been impoverishing and limiting and holding down this world and holding captive these people these many centuries may all be snapped and broken, that the people may hear the truths and come into Thy Kingdom.

<u>November 18, 1965</u>: President Jesperson met with a young couple named Brother and Sister Oswaldo Espinosa from La Merced which lies a couple of hours into the jungle from Tarma, Peru. Sister Espinosa is a Brazilian. They are living in La Merced and want us to send missionaries into there to begin a branch. Sister Espinosa said she has converted many couples to the Church. There are about 10,000 people in La Merced; mostly of the indigenous race.

President Sterling Nicolaysen summarized the three years of his mission as follows:

"The first year was a time of growth in member leadership, calling, and capacitating -- giving first experience to local leaders. We just progressively went through the branches that had already been organized under President Sharp's administration; getting local leaders established at all points in the branch structure, and undertook our first district organization. We organized the Lima District and transferred control from the mission home and began to regard the mission home as the general level, because with the mission office under the direct supervision of the Quorum of the Twelve, they really do represent the general level of Church government.

So, we set up the district organization and advanced in branch organization and began to wean the people from such complete reliance on the mission boards so that the materials and training that did come out of the mission office were not all products of North Americans. Some of that development occurred in the first year, even to the mission board level.

In the second year, we went ahead with a little more sophistication to the Church and to help them learn to develop and train each other. We spent a great deal of effort on standardized training programs. While we had some patterns in this from things we learned in our regional mission conferences, we took the responsibility for preparing our own training programs.

I had the help of some really excellent missionary assistants on this who could do the work of executive secretaries. They really functioned in that way. There were some outstanding elders in that regard -- three of them in particular. They really ought to be in the history. Of course they are, but there were Elder Joseph H. Groberg and David Smith. Before either of them, Donald Lynn Jones, who remained for a short time with me after President Tuttle left. Elder Jones had been instructed by President Tuttle and as prepared to follow up on the material from President Tuttle which I was unable to absorb completely in our first orientation. Lynn Jones first, Joseph Groberg, David Smith, and Carl Hunt later -- these are young men who, in some cases, came from families that are quite prominent in missionary work and who, just by background, innate capacity, and family experience seemed to be able to capture ideas quickly. During the writing of the training programs, David Smith, who spent all of his mission in the mission office, was especially helpful. I've never had a period when there seemed to be more input form the Spirit to help us outline and see the structure of things as they were to evolve.

I should go ahead with the third year. If that second year was a period of refinement and more sophistication and in-depth development and a more thorough effort to provide training programs, the third year was a time when, with additional missionaries and some additional budget for opening new branches, we took the Church and the proselytizing program into virgin territory. We did a lot of reconnaissance work in the mountain areas trying to determine where we would begin our work away from the coast -- in which community, with what strength of missionaries.

I'm aware of these cycles that occur. You surge ahead and then you discover your foundation isn't strong enough and you retrench. I can see by reading the Church Directory through the years that there have been missionaries presiding in branches in Peru where we established local leaders. If you interviewed President Jesperson, who succeeded me, and he had to characterize his first year in the mission field, he might have to say, "Well, it was a time of consolidation." We discovered we were over-extended. We had people who had titles, but didn't have understanding. They held offices but didn't have skills, background, and faith.

They probably felt that we got rather reckless in our organizing, but I don't have anxieties about that, because I think it's all part of the process and had to occur. As I look back, I don't think we did anything too fast. I wish we could have done it more thoroughly with even more understanding, but I just don't feel that anything was done recklessly or too fast. Even if some of the members failed, I think it was essential that they have a chance. We had very, very good experiences in our efforts to capacitate the people, and of course in that kind of country it's a significant part of a Mission Presidents work.

Yungay, at the base of Peru's highest mountain, Huascaran, was the place where a rather rabid, fanatical priest whipped up innocent, but ignorant and backward local resident Indians -- people from the surrounding villages -- in some opposition to the Church. They had an interesting experience documenting the visit of hostile spirits, angels of the devil, who actually spoke aloud their intentions.

We probed this question: what do you do if you go into an area to serve before you presume to proselyte too heavily, feeling that with a lot of needs, people were not ready for a high degree of Gospel teaching until they could at least concurrently have some help in improving their physical conditions. (Alma-Aaron.)

We had a very enlightened member, who figures I'm sure in the written mission history, Hugo Fiedler. He had left the Vanadium Corporation and established a little chicken ranch in a very, very rustic village near Ambo, Peru. And Ambo was down the valley from Huanuco, which would be the closest provincial town that I can note. I had been told about him by the lady missionaries who converted him in Lima. When I first met him, I could see that he was an advanced thinker who had aspirations to do things for his people. He made his little chicken ranch a community center, and he treated his employees differently and had an interest in getting them into better housing and so forth. We finally evolved -- and undoubtedly, the history would show it involved thinking with President

Tuttle, who naturally was visionary this way, and also communicated with Elder Kimball -- we evolved the plan for sending some elders up there who would really spend time with the people. This was, by no means, meant to be an imitation of the Peace Corps, and in practice it definitely was not. But we did plan that these elders would have to take off their suit trousers and put on khakis and boots and spend time with the people. With the help of some contributions that we received from interested people here in the States and through contacts that Elder Kimball made available, we established a little workshop in this community. The elders taught the people how to make some furniture. They took young boys into the shop and helped them to make chairs and tables, and I think in a couple of cases with another stringer, and then some cross pieces, poles coming from the wall to this first platform piece to form the equivalent of a bed, and they threw on those poles, skins, hides, or something, and slept that way. But they had no table and no chairs. Didn't have the food -- in other words, up off of the floor when they ate it. And these are people who live in little mud houses without windows; in many cases, with one opening to enter and maybe one vent some place for some of the cooking smokes to be exhausted. People who kept guinea pigs in the house as a source of good, with chickens and guinea pigs running in and out.

The name for this kind of a little farm "<u>Granja Siete</u>", it was called because Brother Fiedler had seven children and a number of other things of consequence in his life that all happened around the number seven.

I'd say we had quite a bit of experience with efforts to get the people helping themselves, to improve themselves economically.

Maybe it can be said it gave us some insights into the modifications that have to be made in the Church program when you go into the backward areas. We had Sister Fiedler come down to Lima and talked to her about what had to be done with the women. She was a woman whose ties were all in the city. It was at the home she maintained in a suburb in Lima that the family had first been met and converted. Her heart was three-quarters in the city and only one-quarter in the hills. But she was converted enough at the time to respond to our promptings and urgings, and at some sacrifice to herself she entered into this program of teaching the ladies how to bathe babies and how to prepare little layettes so that there would be clean clothing for the babies when they were born. We tried to do some of the thinking that would make the Relief Society program meaningful to people of that culture and level."

He also spoke of a special building program and the challenges involved in the construction of buildings:

"You see the custom there is that people not soil their hands. The people will strain to avoid any appearance of being in the laboring class. So we had sisters of very humble means who couldn't bring themselves to go down and cook and wash dishes at the building project. Even though they were people in humble circumstances, they hired help to do these things for themselves in their own homes. It took a lot of humility to go shop and to go down and prepare food at the building project. This was a real hurdle for the people to overcome. We, of course, had North Americans -- wives of the building supervisors -- who modeled the desired behavior. But what we did wasn't entirely helpful to the local people because they knew we were from a different culture and that it was acceptable for us. They were among their neighbors and effort of this kind still reflected on them.

This general pattern was made evident to me in a couple of ways. If a man came to paint in the mission home, he never came dressed in working clothes. The humblest man living in a little home where there was no plumbing and no facilities would still get dressed up in clothes that looked like dress-up clothes and come on a bicycle, or maybe by other means of transportation, but after he arrived at the mission home he would change, and before he ever left his work he would change back into his other clothes.

One of our Branch Presidents was from a fairly prominent family in the north, but again of limited means. He told me how he went to Lima once to work and took work on a construction project carrying concrete or blocks, menial labor, and he met a friend who was doing the same work, and they made a solemn pact that neither of them would ever reveal to anybody that they had seen each other in this condition doing that kind of work.

This means then that to tell the Relief Society Sister that she was responsible for seeing that the purchase of the food was assigned and accomplished and then that a cook, if she were placed on the project, was supervised and instructed, you knew you were giving a real challenge to that Relief Society. They couldn't always succeed in getting people to fill this kind of assignment. We had some very difficult times when our building supervisors' wives would have to fill in."

The major focus, of course, was the regular proselytizing work. President Nicolaysen explained his major challenges in that aspect:

"We attempted to implement what is really the Priesthood Missionary Program in magnifying members and their referrals, although some of our emphasis was on obtaining referrals from investigators and very recent converts. I can remember spending a lot of time in missionary meetings explaining the spiritual condition of the new convert, the intensity of his feelings and his awareness of what he was experiencing and what the Lord had helped him do to get a testimony, and how his readiness to give referrals contrasted with the attitude of a member who was nine months away from his point of conversion. So we attempted to magnify the investigator, the man who was in the process of conversion and process the referrals that would come from a current investigator or a very recent convert.

I still believe that if we do a proper job of helping a new convert enter into missionary work at that very time, we might establish a pattern that will carry over into his later years in Church service, but if you miss that opportunity at the point of conversion to get the referrals that are available then, you deprive a member of his first experiences in member missionary work.

The first member counselor to the Mission President was President Vidal who had served as the first local Member President of the Miraflores Branch in Lima."

On being released, President Nicolaysen said,

"So we just quietly returned to our home and set about the problems of trying to figure out what to do. I think we just lived through what the other missionary elders and lady missionaries experience. At first you are very involved, and you can't be anywhere without letting a companion know where you are or why you are there. But when the release finally comes, you don't have to account to anybody and nobody's counting on you, and you just go home. It's a very melancholy, empty period. It is a very difficult period. That's not to suggest that we don't appreciate the opportunities for service here at home and the significance of them. And it's not to suggest that we crave status, position of importance, feel deflated. It's just the emptiness of having been so close to so many people for so long. It's such an intense period of service, full-time involvement in the work, and then suddenly being back in the world of bread and butter, with more fleeting experiences in the Church. We all commit to maintain a program of study, of personal challenge. But the degree of spirituality weakens."

January 8, 1966: The trip over the Andes to Huancayo goes over the highest standard gauge railroad in the world at 15, 681 feet.

January 9, 1966: The Huancayo Branch was organized with Elder Willes as Branch President, Brother Javier as First Counselor, Brother Vega as Second Counselor and Brother Rojas as Branch Clerk. This is the first time that local members have been in the Branch Presidency. Huancayo is situated in a large valley.

On February 22, 1966: Quillabamba, in Peru, also opened to missionary work.

October 12, 1966: La Prensa Daily Newspaper of Lima, Peru:

CHILDREN OF ANY CREED WILL BE ADMITTED IN THE MORMON SCHOOL. The creation of a school in Lima for children for any religion was made known by the Andean Mission for the coming year by the Church of Jesus Christ of Latter-Day Saints (Mormon). The Andean Mission has 240 branches in Bolivia, Ecuador, and Chile. Their aim is to preach their doctrine by individual betterment, cultural, social, educational, and economic. Students of primary and secondary age will be admitted and will not have to receive obligatory religious instruction.

December 31, 1966: 1,350 baptisms this year; 1,150 in 1965.

February 17, 1967: Sister Jesperson and I left for Ica, Peru to be with the Branch Presidency and members this weekend. We stopped in Paracas on the day down. Our purpose was to visit the "Tree of Life", so named by our missionaries, that is carved on a cliff at the ocean edge. One can only see the carving from the ocean, so it was necessary for us to charter a boat for the trip.

February 18, 1967: After a short night's rest, we rented a boat with a family of Peruvians and went to sea. From the landing to the area where the tree can be seen took approximately 45 minutes. The natives call the caring a candelabra and indeed it does resemble this about as much as a tree. There are certain features, however, that make it appear to us who know the story of the Tree of Life, that it really is a tree and not a candelabra.

March 27, 1967: I had a report from my assistant, Elder Marc Haws, from Huaraz, Peru that the mayor, the governor and the chief of police had written a letter requesting that the Mormons and all the missionaries leave the town of Huaraz. The excuse they gave for this expulsion was that two of our missionaries had turned their backs on a Catholic procession on Good Friday and that in so doing, they had acted irreverently, offended and insulted the townspeople. It appears the elders had actually done this, but in complete ignorance. I asked Elder Haws to go to the governor, mayor and chief of police and whoever else it might be necessary to go to and apologize and explain to them it was not our intent to in any way offend them.

May 17, 1967: Elder Gordon B. Hinckley arrived and spoke at a conference in Lima on the need of accepting the responsibility in the Church and magnifying the calls given and how converts have been blessed beyond their imagination when they had accepted and magnified the calling they received.

July 16, 1967: The official inauguration of the Comas Branch in Lima took place this evening at the Sacrament Meeting. The hall was completely filled with several standing in the door to the rear. We were thrilled with the successful meeting and feel confident that the Comas Branch will grow rapidly.

November 19, 1967: Two new branches have been opened in the last week or so. The Trujillo Branch has been reopened in a different part of the city, and the Chimbote Branch in the city of Chimbote, Peru, 120 kilometers south of Trujillo. A total of 1,673 baptisms for all of 1967.

In June 1968, Elder Harold B. Lee talked about his experiences in organizeing the Andes Mission and said, "I remember standing at the pulpit in the archway between the living room and the dining room. As I spoke to the congregation, I was impressed bythe Spirit of the Lord, in a way in which I had seldom been impressed before, to tell the people that the land of Peru had been one of the most important lands in all the history and development of the people of the Book of Mormon." He subsequently commented that he wondered if Lehi and his family had perhaps landed on or near the coasts of Peru."

July 24, 1968: President and Sister Allen Litster and their daughter, Melanie, arrived in Lima early this morning. At about midnight, the Jespersons left for Mexico on their return trip back to California.

January 11, 1969: President and Sister Litster flew to Huanuco to attend the Annual Conference of the Huanuco Branch. A branch dinner activity was held Saturday evening as was a leadership meeting. During the dinner, Brother John Morales, member of the Branch Presidency, commented that he works as the Radio Operator and Meteorologist at the Huanaco Airport. He said that the Airline Company had contacted him from Lima that morning asking for weather clearance in order to fly to Huanuco. He said that he realized that the weather was not good enough to fly but then he thought "Now, the President of the Andes Mission is going to be on that plane, and if he is going to be on it, there should be no trouble getting here." After that comment, President and Sister Litster understood better why they had been flying in such dense clouds with rocky mountain peaks all around them. Incidentally, the plane they were flying in was not radar-equipped.

March 30, 1969: Today the Peruvian North District (Distrito Nor-Peruano) was organized at a special meeting held for members of the Chiclayo, Piura and Cajamarca Branches in the chapel in Chiclayo. Those three branches will comprise the district. Elder David E. Logie was called and sustained as the District President.

April 24, 1969 (Thursday): Today Elder Hinckley met with the missionaries from the Quito and Guayaquil Zones at the Villa Flora Chapel. As Elder Hinckley bore witness of the divinity of the Savior and mentioned his great love for Him, he wept openly as did most of the missionaries present. Elder Hinckley also told the missionaries that he felt that the spirits of some of the great ancient American Prophets had been present at that meeting, inasmuch as they are interested in seeing that their descendants receive the message of the restored Gospel. The Spirit bore witness to those who were present that the Lord had indeed spoken through one of his special witnesses and that the feelings which Elder Hinckley had expressed were true and correct.

After the meeting, Elder Hinckley and President Litster went to the President's Palace where an appointment had been made with President Jose Maria Velasco Ibarra. The President was unable to see them at the appointed time and the secretary asked the visitors to return later. When they returned they were taken into the Palace and into the secretary's office where they were informed that it would be impossible for the

President to see them. Some of the missionaries began to try to plead with the man to let Elder Hinckley see the President. President Litster had the impression that an Apostle of the Lord need not beg nor plead to see any government officer.

Elder Hinckley immediately agreed and stated that it is impossible for a man to ignore and slight the servants of the Lord and continue to receive the sustaining power of the Lord in his position. He commented that those present would watch the future of the man who had turned them away, and would see it begin to decline because of what had happened that day, that by refusing to assist the servants of the Lord to accomplish their righteous purposes, they had incurred the wrath of a just God.

June 1, 1969: The first member of the Iquitos Branch to be ordained an Elder, Brother Jose Roger Pinto, was sustained by the members of the Branch and ordained by President Litster following the meeting.

July 8, 1969: President Jose Sousa, first counselor in the mission presidency, was involved in an accident while traveling in the Callejon de Huaylays in the mountains of Peru. As he drove along the winding road, his eyes tricked him while in what he thought to be a straight section of highway but what turned out to be a twenty meter drop into the river. Brother Sousa blacked out as the car went over the cliff, and the next thing he remembers is when he was brought to his senses by the icy water filling the cab of the car. Panic-stricken, he struggled to escape from the car. It was useless, however, for the door had been so severely damaged in the fall that it could not be opened. He was drowning. Then he recalled the great power which he possessed and silently prayed that if it were the Lord's will that he be saved, to grant him the faith he needed. Calming himself as much as possible, he commanded that he be permitted to leave, by virtue of the Priesthood which he held, and by the power thereof. No sooner had he commanded this than he pushed the door as hard as he could and it swung open, allowing him to escape. All of this took place in a few seconds, and he found himself clinging to the top of the truck, inches above the surface of the icy, fast moving water. His hands became numb as the current tried to drag him away from his grip on the edge of the roof. Was he to drown after being saved once? His cries for help were soon answered by someone far above on the bridge. "Is anyone alive down there?" "Hello, hello!" "Get a rope," he cried, "I can't hang on much longer." "I don't have a rope in the truck," was the reply, but then the truck drivers assisistant said, "I think I put one in this trip; I don't know why, but I did." They lowered the rope, which barely left enough slack to tie around his waist and pull him up.

A series of coincidences? One would have a hard time convincing Brother Sousa of that. He has seen the power of the Priesthood and the power of prayer in action.

<u>October 5, 1969:</u>   For the first time the members of the Church in Peru listened to the transmission of General Conference from Salt Lake City, Utah.

Chapter 9

The First Stake & the Earthquake

The few days from February 14 to February 22, 1970, brought significant spiritual experiences to the Andes Mission. On Saturday, February 14, the District Leader in Huanuco called to report that one of the Elders was seriously ill. The doctor in whose home the missionaries lived had treated him for Paratyphoid, but he had continued to grow worse. Impressed that something was seriously wrong, President Lister told the District Leader to ensure that the Elder was on the airplane that day to Lima. When the plane arrived that afternoon, he was too weak to walk and had to be carried from the plane. That evening Pres. Lister visited him at the hospital and gave him a blessing. Tests indicated a sever internal infection of unkown origin. Each day he grew weaker. His fellow missionaries fasted and prayed for his recovery. By Tuesday evening he could barely speak and often only the whites of his eyes were visible. Dr. Belaochaga asked permission for emergency surgery to pinpoint the source of the infection and possibly save the Elder's life. In a blessing given to the Elder just prior to the surgery, Pres. Lister was impressed to quote the Lord's promise to missionaries in D&C 84:88, ". . . I will go before your face. I will be on your right hand and on your left, and my Spirit shall be in your hearts, and min angels round about you to bear you up." The surgeon finished about midnight and reported that they had found a ruptured appendix -- probably ruptured for ten days. It was located on the left side and under the pelvic bone where it was hidden from the X-Rays, making it impossible to diagnose without surgery. The surgeon said, "He is young and strong; I think he has a 50% chance to survive." A little later, as Pres. Lister sat down quietly at his bedside, the Elder weakly motioned for him to come very close. He whispered, "President, there were angels there."

For three days the missionary hovered between life and death. Each day Pres. Lister, assisted by other missionaries, gave him a blessing, and with each blessing there was an immediate increase in his strength and alertness.

On Thursday, Elder A. Theodore Tuttle arrived in the mission and upon learning of the missionary's condition, asked to go to the hospital. The Elder could barely whisper and his eyes were rolled back in his head when they entered the room. A priesthood blessing was lovingly given, and again there was an immediate improvement. As they left, Elder Tuttle commented that he had never seen such an immediate and remarkable response to a priesthood blessing. He added, "President Lister, you bless that young man as often as you have to in order to keep him alive." Within ten days, much to the surpise of the doctors, the elder was released from the hospital and, after a few weeks of recovery, returned to full missionary service.

Elder Gordon B. Hinckley arrived in Lima on Friday, February 20 for the purpose of organizing the Lima Peru Stake. Assisted by Elder Tuttle and President Lister, Elder Hinkley interviewed the presidency of the Lima Central District as well as the branch presidents and other local Church officers. The leaders were all deeply touched by the gentle yet thorough interviews they each had with this wonderful Apostle of the Lord. None of them were found unworthy, but it was clearly manifested by the Lord who should serve as the first president of the Lima Peru Stake, the first to be organized in the western part of South America.

<u>February 22, 1970:</u>   This morning the quarterly conference of the Lima General District was held in the chapel at Limatambo. <u>Elder Gordon B. Hinckley</u> of the Council of the Twelve was presiding, assisted by <u>Elder A. Theodore Tuttle</u> of the First Council of the Seventy. President Litster directed the meeting. The Lima Stake was organized with the following officers and officials: President Robert Vidal; Jose Armando

Sousa, 1st counselor; Harold M. Rex, 2nd counselor; Manuel Paredes, Stake Clerk; Constancion Chinchay and Melquiades Vilchez, Assistant Clerks; J. Lynn Gubler, Executive Secretary, and High Council members as follows: Luis Jimeno, Gerald Stubbs, Carlos Figala, Jorge Tejada, Alejandro Robles, Salvador Garcia, Lloyd Burnett, Emilio Giraldo, and Lucio Lazo. Thus the Lima Stake of Zion came into existence, the 503rd of the Church. The following is part of the talk given by Elder Hinckley:

> The Stake is organized, and now the work begins. Now I should like to repeat to you the promise given through revelation to those who help His servants, that they shall in no wise lose their reward. Now, I do not hesitate to promise you as a servant of the Lord, that as you do so you will bring blessings upon your heads, a sweetness and joy such as you have never known.
>
> I look into the faces of you people and I see the blood of those who walked this land anciently, and who at that time found great favor with the Lord, but because of wickedness and indulgence they lost that favor. Because of their wickedness they were oppressed and driven and killed. I also see forebearers of others who are here today. There is in the veins of hundreds who sit here a mixture of those two great people, the descendants of Father Lehi that found favor in the sight of God, and the Spanish who came here in the name of Christianity.
>
> Now I would like to say to you today that you are a people of prophecy, and this is a day of fulfilled prophecy, and God is remembering the promises made of old. If you will be humble, and prayerful and devoted, He will magnify and honor you and bless you in your basket and in your store. He will bless you in faith and testimony. He will magnify you before your associates in the Church and out of the Church. He will bring peace into your homes, joy into your lives, progress in your development. You will

be a blessed and happy people. But without faithfulness you cannot expect those blessings. If you fail to keep the commandments you will wither in your faith, your testimonies will shrivel, and you will be an unhappy people. Consider the alternatives. The choice is yours...

The men who have been called to preside have been selected by the Lord. But they are not the only ones who have been called. Every man and woman who sits in this hall this day; every man, woman and child who has entered the waters of baptism is called and has an obligation as serious, terms of responsibility.... Whereas too there are thousands in Lima, in the near future there will be tens of thousands.

May 31, 1970: After the Stake Conference, Elder Hinckley quickly hurried to the airport. However, his plane was an hour and a half late so he and President Lister utilized the time to discuss Church business matters. At 3:23 p.m. Sunday Afternoon, his plane had scarcely left the ground when Peru was stricken with the biggest disaster it had known in recent years.

June 1, 1970 (Monday): It was reported that Chimbote, where four of our missionaries were located, was seventy percent destroyed, with heavy damage in Trujillo, where another eight missionaries labored. Telephone and cable lines were down and thieves began to carry off the downed lines. Communications were limited to ham radio operators and private company radios. Then on Monday afternoon, urgent pleas began to come in through small private radios located in the beautiful Callejon de Huaylas, a narrow, deep valley located in Central Peru, over which towers Mount Huascaran, Peru's highest peak. They reported extensive damage, ninety percent of the city of Huaraz destroyed, the survivors among its thirty-five thousand (35,000) inhabitants having fled in terror to the surrounding hillsides. Caraz, a city of some twelve thousand (12,000) had reportedly disappeared from the map, completely wiped out. Our concern increased as we considered the missionaries laboring in each of those cities and the some one hundred (100) church members living there. All the missionaries were safe, none of the one hundred seventy members had been seriously injured, though six families had lost their homes.

June 2, 1970: By Tuesday morning the estimated death toll had climbed to 5,000. The church van was loaded with 130 blankets, three cases of medicines donated by another local member, Milton Jay Berrey, who manages a drug company; 8 cases of canned milk; 3 cases of bread and provisions for the five missionaries selected for the trip. (Richard Fairbanks, who had been to both cities; David Thompson, a professional builder; Paul Newman, a former survival instructor; Leslie Roberts, registered nurse; Mary Louise Rojas, calm capable lady missionary.)

They left Lima at 5:00 p.m. representing our only hope for communication with the missionaries. Their instructions were to try to get an airlift into the Callejon de Huaylas as soon as the airport was repaired enough to permit landing there. They were to care for the injured and evacuate any injured missionaries. Realizing the grim nature of the situation, burial clothing was also sent in with them.

June 3, 1970: On Wednesday, at 2:00 a.m., Elder Fairbanks called by radio through the power company from Chimbote. They had arrived safely but there was little hope of getting the group or the supplies on into the Callejon de Huaylas. Perhaps there was a very remote possibility that one of them could get in on a helicopter the next morning if the helicopters could get in through the heavy overcast and the tremendous dust cloud raised by the earthquake and resulting land slides.

Elder Gordon B. Hinckley returned from Rio de Janeiro, Brazil. When he had learned on Monday that we had no word from the four missionaries in the Callejon de Huaylas, he advised us that he was going to come back to Lima. He said he didn't feel right about going back to Salt Lake City while there were still missionaries missing.

Wednesday morning, the estimated death toll had now risen to 30,000. Still no word from the missionaries in Caraz and Huaraz, things began to look more and more unfavorable. A radio phone call came from Elder Richard Openshaw in Chimbote. The Elders were sleeping in the park. Elder Fairbanks, Elder Newman and two of the President's Assistants, Elder Richard Gillespie and Elder David Fales, who had been in the area when the quake occurred, had left early Wednesday morning with a guide to hike into Huaraz, no hope for going in by plane. They hoped to arrive there by Thursday evening. They only had to go fifty miles as the crow flies, but that distance was practically doubled by what was left of the winding road.

So far, the only help into Callejon de Huaylas had come from 30 paratroopers who had jumped in Tuesday afternoon. Frantic cries for help continued to stream from the Callejon de Huaylas. People were dying from simple injuries just because there was no one to take care of them. Aerial photos showed nothing but rubble and massive mud slides.

For a long time there were no ways to get information in or out of the Callejon de Huaylas.. There were two lady missionaries in the group, one of them a registered nurse. As the rescue team of missionaries with a small truck with emergency supplies approached the Callejon, the destruction forced them to halt the truck as there were no roads in which to further penetrate the area. Neither were there messages coming out of the area. Four elders of the rescue team then hiked to Huaraz on foot, taking only two days to hike the more than seventy kilometers -- about forty-five miles -- over terrain that had been disrupted by the earthquake. Most of these kilometers were straight up the side of the mountains.

Meanwhile the missionaries in Lima began a fast for the success of the rescue group and for the safety of the missionaries and the members. Three days had passed without any news of them. Only two hours into the fast, the U.S. Airforce Colonel who had flown the elders in Caraz to Chimbote called to report their safety. Colonel Beckett called the mission office and said Elder Michael Nielsen and Elder Allen Arvig were OK. "I flew a chopper in there today to study the possibilities for rebuilding the landing strip; they did some translating for me. They are well and happy, wondering if they could help more where they are or somewhere else." When President Litster walked out of the office and shared the news with the some ten missionaries waiting in the outer office. Tears began to flow freely. Missionaries hugged each other. Some ran to tell others who waited in other parts of the building. Voices choked up. Then, at 10:30 pm that same evening, the radio reported a message, "Attention Lima. Attention Lima. Mormon missionaries in Huaraz are well. We repeat. Mormon missionaries in Huaraz are well." The tears flowed again, more hugs, more scurrying to share the news. Elder Kent Toone and Elder Ladd Walkins were safe. Grateful prayers welled up in the hearts of everyone.

Now, of the miraculous happenings of which there are many, one of the most interesting was the way the Lord's hand sustained the Saints in spite of the many, many people who were killed (approximately 70,000). There were 170 members in Chimbote, 85 other members in the Callejon de Huaylas (a river valley, bordered by mountains, which contained the cities of Caraz, Huaraz, Yungay and Chimbote), and over 900 members in Trujillo. Yet, in spite of all the destruction, there were only two members, apparently, that lost their lives, and two others that were injured -- a man from Chimbote suffered a broken leg and a man in Huaraz had a badly scratched arm.

The two members who died had lived in the city of Yungay and are believed to have been buried in the mud slide that followed the earthquake. Until two weeks before the earthquake, when the elders who had been visiting them occasionally from Caraz had convinced them to go to Sunday School in Caraz, these members had not been active in the Church since 1965 when the missionaries had been run out of Yungay due to the influence and pressure of the Catholic priests. The priests had threatened the people that -- among other things that would happen -- if they didn't get the Mormons out of the city, the mountain was going to fall in on them. One group of non-Mormons in Yungay came to the defense of the missionaries. In a local paper, these people published a statement of their defense, declared the right of the missionaries to be there and their right for freedom of religion, and signed their names to the article. Eventually, however, the missionaries left.

During the days that followed the earthquake, in which more than 20,000 of the 25,000 people in Yungay were killed, lists of survivors were broadcast from the stricken areas. One Elder in Lima, looking through the mission history of Yungay while monitoring these broadcasts for the names of the missionaries in these areas, told the mission president, "An interesting thing is happening. I was just reading about these people who published their defense of the missionaries. These same names are coming out on the survivor lists from Yungay!"

The Lord's hand was made manifest in every part of the affected region. After the earthquake the elders walked to the chapel over the eight feet of debris. At first they passed it by because it was unrecognizable from the debris. The building that we used in Caraz was one of the few left largely intact. There were cracks in the walls and you could see daylight in the corners. But the building was standing. In Huaraz, the building was completely destroyed except for the chapel part where the piano, pulpit, sacrament table, benches, and things like that were. Although all the rest of it was laid flat -- we even had to dig the records out from under eight feet of adobe -- the major furnishings were not scratched.

The only damage to the building in Chimbote was the fall of a piece of ceiling plaster about eighteen inches square. A wall from the building next door fell against a window of the chapel and just slid down the side, not breaking a thing. Across the street a two-story reinforced concrete school was all buckled and twisted. In Trujillo, where ten percent of the buildings were completely destroyed and twenty percent more were damaged, our chapel wasn't hurt at all.

Many of the streets in Huaraz are so narrow that the wheels of a car rub both curbs. At the time of the earthquake, the missionaries were teaching a man on one of the two streets in all of the city that was not later filled with eight to ten feet of debris -- mostly bricks and cement that fell. The house where the elders lived was destroyed except for their room which was left in tact. A similar thing happened in Chimbote.

The Friday after the earthquake, the missionaries helped a Peace Corps volunteer locate the bodies of two Peace Corps girls. It was a very sad task. They found them, wrapped in each other's arms, under the debris in the street where they had apparently fled. Their remains were placed in plastic bags and buried on a beautiful hillside overlooking Huaraz. Such was the fate of many people. In the clean-up process, 175 bodies were uncovered in one block. The ambulance could get no closer to the Plaza de Armas than eight blocks; there was no where it could go but along the outskirts of the tow.

The significance of the earthquake for the members of the Church of Jesus Christ of Latter-day Saints is far greater than just another happening in the course of nature. The prophets of Old saw these, the last days. Nephi spoke of these times over five hundred years before Christ: We recognize the proximity of the second coming of the Lord and bear witness that these signs of the times reflect just that.

But, behold, in the last days, or in the days of the Gentiles -- yea behold all the nations of the Gentiles and also the Jews, both those who shall come upon this land and those who shall be upon other lands, yea, even upon all the lands of the earth, behold, they will be drunken with iniquity and all manner of abominations –

And when that day shall come they shall be visited of the Lord of Hosts, with thunder and with earthquake, and with a great noise, and with storm, and with tempest, and with the flame of devouring fire. (2 Nephi 27: 1, 2)

Symbolizing the faith and determination of the members of the church, the following letter dated June 5, 1970, from one of the members living in Caraz, was translated and included herein:

Dear President Litster:

I write you these lines to greet you, your wife, and the brothers and sisters in Lima, at the same time thanking you for the thirty-one blankets that you so generously sent to us, your brothers and sisters in Caraz, who find ourselves in difficult circumstances. I thank you on behalf of all of the members and hope our Heavenly Father will bless you richly.

Personally, Brother Litster, I am very, very grateful to my dear Heavenly Father for the goodness and mercy that He has shown and does show toward me and toward all my family and towards the members of the Caraz Branch. He has saved us from dying among the ruins; my testimony of the truthfulness of our Church grows because in these critical moments my Heavenly Father has given us and continues to give us more spiritual strength. Difficult and sad have been these tragic moments, but the spirit of the Lord is and has been with us to protect us. Truly, the city of Caraz is in ruins except for a few homes that are still standing but badly cracked. Our dear meetinghouse has not been so totally affected; we hope to be able to have Sunday School this Sunday in the patio as well as testimony meeting. It is marvelous, brother, that I can feel the Spirit of the Lord during my prayers in these tragic days as I do in this moment with such fervor that it causes me to shed tears. Oh, my brother, I have no doubt that God the Father and Jesus Christ live and that we are in their true Church. The members and missionaries have not even received a scratch because of the earthquake. Elders Nielson and Arvig went to Huaraz in a helicopter to look for the other Elders. We are worried because we know nothing about them, but we trust in God that they are alive and well.

Truly, my brother, I think that the Callejon has been chastised for not having accepted the message of the Church of Jesus Christ due to the idolatry of the people. I know that Huaraz is going to be burned and perhaps Caruhas as well. Yungay has totally disappeared while in Caraz, though in ruins, the major part of its inhabitants have been saved. Yesterday we had a public meeting and all the people are optimistic about reconstructing the city of Caraz. All the men fifteen years old and above get together in large battalions with their shovels, picks and crowbars in order to construct within a few days another landing strip and thus be able to receive greater help and thus get out of the desperate state in which we find ourselves. I have cried a great deal as I see the city in ruin, but I have confidence and faith in our Heavenly Father, that He is preparing something important for the progress of His Kingdom on earth. I also hope with all my heart that this test the Lord has sent us will not cause the Caraz Branch to be closed but rather, as we were planning Sunday with the Elders in the monthly Primary preparation meeting just minutes before the earthquake, we are committed to teach the message of the Primary of the Church of Jesus Christ to the lame, the blind, the poor, now that the chosen ones have rejected it.

Brother Litster, I would be the saddest person on earth if our dear Caraz Branch were closed. It is certain that the people here are very, very hard, but I am sure that there are many people who have an open heart, though their traditions and prejudices such as "What will the people say?" prohibit them from accepting the gospel and being members of the true Church. The Elders have worked hard, but I think, brother, that in Caraz one must struggle with the very forces of the devil who is here in strength. Nevertheless, I am sure that the forces of Jesus Christ are stronger and I believe that the Elders and members should not be weak at any moment.

I should tell you that all the survivors from the city of Caraz are living in tents made of blankets, others from branches. Thus far, with the blessing of our Heavenly Father, we are not yet suffering hunger because we receive indispensable daily food rations. The government is sending help in medicines, foods, etc., but it is arriving in small quantities because the helicopters will carry very little. We are now calmer and I have great faith in our Heavenly Father that within a short while things will be better. I plead with you to pray for us so that no epidemic may break out among us and so that Lake Paron may not break and spill over.

With all my love of the gospel, Your sister, Elsa Ruth Alba R.

P. S. Many affectionate greetings from the members of the Caraz Branch. Though we are afflicted, we have the Spirit of the Lord to console us. The members are saddened because of the loss of one of the unbaptized daughters of Sister Barrios. They plan to go to Lima. The Ramirez family is also intending to go to Chimbote. I intend to stay here because of my work.

FOLLOWING ARE EXCERPTS FROM AN INTERVIEW HELD WITH ELDER GORDON B. HINCKLEY OF THE COUNCIL OF THE TWELVE IN WHICH ELDER MICHAEL B. NIELSEN, PRESIDENT OF THE CARAZ BRANCH, AND HIS COMPANION, ELDER ALLEN ARVIG, TOLD OF THEIR EXPERIENCES IN THE EARTHQUAKE OF MAY 31, 1970 IN WHICH THE TOWN OF CARAZ WAS GREATLY DESTROYED. *Elder Arvig: Marine Corp Vietnam War Veteran

Elder Arvig*: We were just about done with the planning meeting (for Primary) -- I believe we had just had our prayers -- when all of a sudden the floor felt like it was going to fall out from under us. I suggested we get up in the window sill. My companion noticed that the wall was wiggling, so he suggested that we go down to the patio. When we got down to the patio we realized that we were surrounded by four big walls that all looked like they were going to fall on us. But to get out of the building we had to go under an underpass, so we stayed there until the earthquake was over. And at that time we all knew that the Lord was really with us because the building truly should have fallen. Being a two-story building, it was really a miracle that it didn't fall.

The earthquake lasted for about a minute, then we went out to the street. We couldn't see much because the dust had risen up all around from all the houses falling and you could see maybe three or four feet ahead of you. The sister that we were with started crying. She grabbed both of our hands and we all started running up to the house to see if her mother was okay. As we were running we had to climb over walls and different things that had fallen. The people were just running all around the city crying and they didn't know what they were doing. Having been in Vietnam, I've seen families cry before, and I've seen little kids hurt before, but that was nothing like this, because in this case there was nothing they could do about it. Every single person in the city was crying and you knew that there were dead people all around you.

I personally felt inside at this time that we were extremely blessed. I was very fortunate to have such a wonderful spiritual companion, one that always seems to have the Spirit with him.

Well, we went up to the house and couldn't find the family, so we went up the mountain to look for them. Then we realized that the lake up above Caraz had most likely broken and was going to flood the city. So we left this sister and ran back down to the city to warn the people and to try to get the people up to the mountains. The lake didn't break, but the lake down below us did, and because of this . . . just about every person in Yungay was killed. As we flew over and looked at Yungay today, it was just impossible to recognize. It looks like a big riverbed completely covered with mud.

Elder Nielsen: The only two things that I could recognize in the whole city were two palm trees that reached above the mud in the Plaza de Armas and the cemetery. My companion and I have reminisced many times about how grateful we were that we were in the Church at that time. Of all the buildings that we'd walked past and that we'd looked at since then, we can truthfully say that that is the one building in Caraz that is not really damaged. As a matter of fact, it's about the only one that is left in perfect condition.

We ended up spending the first night on the road under our blankets. The second day we piled our blankets up and went to the town once more trying to help. Unfortunately the leaders of the town hadn't accepted our help. We offered many times, but there just wasn't too much we could do. They weren't organized and they didn't really want our help. We did feel really good, though, as we went to bed that first night. As were lying there trying to get some sleep, a man came up and talked to some people that were standing by us. He said, "The gringos are the only men in this town." Although we hadn't done much, he made us feel that tomorrow we'd try harder.

There were five camps where the people have gathered. As the time came to pass out food and distribute it, we really noticed a great difference in the way it was done. Fortunately for us, we ate well -- but then we can contrast it with camp number one that had the mayor and the Catholic authorities. For one breakfast they were eating beef steaks, drinking their wines, and things like this. Twenty yards away people were starving; they would not give them anything to eat. They were sitting on top of their food guarding it so no one would steal it. A lot of people were eating better than they'd ever eaten before in their lives, and many people were going without.

That Wednesday afternoon things started to get hot for us and for the members; the people started saying that the Mormons were to blame and that we should be thrown out from the city and things like that. Wednesday morning when the Elders came out of the tent they had fashioned as a shelter, they found at the entrance a semi-circle of candles, statues and pictures that had been retrieved from the Catholic churches. (Since in the mountains a semi-circle of candles in front of the door of a dwelling is a threat to the life of the owner of the dwelling, the missionaries went back to the airport hoping to get out. A helicopter came in and the co-pilot was a fellow who Elder Arvig had know previously in El Salvador when he had served as a Marine security officer. He explained the situation to his friend who flew them as far as Chimbote where they caught a plane to Lima.)

Elder Arvig: As one of the sisters asked us to lay our hands upon her head and give her a special blessing to give her courage and strength, I remember the feeling that I had fill my body. And at that time I knew that the Lord truly had preserved us and had kept His Spirit with us. These people could kill us physically, but even if we died physically, we would know that once again we would be able to see our Father in Heaven in the flesh.

Elder Gordon B. Hinkley continued asking the Elders about the kind and amount of aid that was needed from the US and how it should be distributed. There was concern about whether it would be welcomed from the church. He concluded his interview with the rescued Elders by saying, "I want to say that I don't know when I've seen a more welcome sight in a long time. This group of missionaries came in looking like anything but missionaries. I'm glad you made it, believe me. I'm so grateful to you, and give you my witness that I think you've been preserved by the hand of the Lord, and I think our people have been preserved by the hand of the Lord, and they will find the Church ready and anxious and alert to help them with their physical needs in this crisis, just as the Church is always ready and anxious to help them with their spiritual needs." The Elders were all ready to return and continue to help as needed.

Elder Arvig: . . . the supplies that we have ordered all can be used very rapidly. But the most important part about it is for us to be there to hand them out and to direct it. I'm sure that the people will realize then that we are really their friends and are trying to help them . . . it may be quite dangerous for us. There's a possibility that we could even lose our lives there. But as we all realize, we're on this earth to help other people and not to think of ourselves. They are fine people. . . . We're being blamed because we're members of the true church.

President Litster: That's it. There's another reason, too. There were missionaries in Yungay as late as 1965, and in 1965 they were run out of Yungay. In part of that process the Catholic priest told the people there that if they didn't run the Mormons out, the mountain was going to fall in on them. Well, you were going back to Yungay once a week to visit members and teach the Gospel and the mountain fell in. Now that's why you're unpopular up there. I had a very interesting conversation with President Sousa just a minute ago and he's been talking with a lot of people about how the Church can help up there. The people in the mountains are highly superstitious people. We know that. And whatever the Catholic priests say is not questioned. That's law to them without any question or reservation, and it's hard to do away with that. No matter how much we might want to do it, we still have to take that into consideration and find a way to give them help by working around these disadvantages.

THE FOLLOWING IS AN ACCOUNT OF THE EARTHQUAKE IN THE CITY OF HUARAZ, PERU, BY ELDER KENT TOONE AND ELDER LADD WILKINS WHO WERE WORKING IN THE AREA AT THE TIME OF THE EARTHQUAKE. ALSO INCLUDED IS AN ACCOUNT OF THE TRIP MADE INTO THE QUAKE AREA BY ELDERS RICHARD GILLESPIE, DAVID FALES, L. PAUL NEWMAN, RICHARD FAIRBANKS, AND DAVID THOMPSON AND SISTERS LESLIE ROBERTS AND MARY RIOJAS. THE CONVERSATION TOOK PLACE IN THE LIVING ROOM OF THE ANDES MISSION HOME JUNE 11, 1970.

Elder Toone: I know the reason we're here today is because the Lord watched over us at that time. During that time between Friday and Saturday there had been some other problems come up that caused me to fast. . . . In the middle of a discussion I remember looking at my companion and telling him, "Let's get out of here." We walked out of the gas station -- and he, the man that we were teaching, followed us out in the street. I remember starting to make a full turn to look at the things that were happening. I made just about half a turn when I saw the mountain to the southeast. It seemed like at least a half a mile of it fell off. A cliff fell loose. The dust that erupted from the falling dirt covered the city for three days. The helicopters couldn't get in because they couldn't see where to land.

It seemed like the earthquake was at its peak. The trembling was so great, I remember I stumbled backwards, and everyone in front of me, my companion included, fell towards me. It almost knocked us off our feet.

The first thing we thought we should do was go to see the members. There was a part-member family that was standing out in the road. They're all girls, a whole family of girls, and they were hysterical. There was a big crowd of people who were running around just trying to get out of the city. They'd all lost their senses; they weren't thinking rationally; they were just plain running as long as they could run.

We went back into the gas station and picked up our stuff that we were giving the charla with and then left. At the time I didn't think that the earthquake had caused much destruction. We saw this little member girl. Her mother was trapped inside the house and she was standing in the door. There was one boy already taking adobes off the place where the mother was. We could see that her leg was trapped. It took us about 20 to 25 minutes to free her. They'd been inside talking, and the member lady, Gudelia Quintana, had gone into the kitchen to fix something. At the moment of the earthquake she'd run back in to get her aunt out of the house. It had taken long enough that they didn't get quite out of the house, so they stopped in the doorway, and that's why they were stuck where they were. This member lady had her foot caught under a kerosene barrel. I was afraid her leg was broken, but it turned out that she was okay.

After we freed her, we started around to visit the other members. We found out that Hermana Vasquez had been seen and was okay. Senor Mallqui had also been seen. We also were asking about our investigators. It seemed like everyone we asked about was okay; not one of them had been hurt.

There was a new subdivision that was being built where we were going to build a school, and that was completely destroyed. We had to climb over rooftops and brick walls that virtually covered the street where we'd once walked. We found out that almost every member on the route had been seen, although we didn't see them.

About 6:30 we went by the church . . . when we got there we walked past it because the blocks were completely unrecognizable. We recognized the church by its painted door. We walked over to the corner of the building where the offices had been. Elder Wilkin's office and my office were buried under more than ten feet of dirt and adobe. My desk was moved clear across the room with enough force to shatter one end of it. The two offices and every classroom were completely ruined, but the chapel itself where we hold the meetings was still intact. The roof was still above it. There were cracks in the wall inside, but nothing had fallen; the piano hadn't been scratched or any of the benches hurt in the least way. Also, the bathroom was okay and the rooms adjacent to the chapel.

It didn't seem like anything could be done there, so we went to our house. Our house was still standing, but the roof was very, very shaky. It was only balanced by a few bricks that were jarred loose. You could see the cracks from the outside in the walls and the bricks were leaning out but the roof was still on. It was getting dark and the members around the city were in the same condition as we were, so we decided we would get our clothes and blankets and take them to the members because the members didn't have anything. All of their houses had fallen while ours was left standing.

With all the dust and the hiking we had done, all we could think of then was that we wanted a drink. We went to the river. It was too filthy. We went back to the place where we were when the earthquake started. Senor Ortiz still had water, so we asked him for a drink. It was one of the two places, or maybe the only place, that had water that night.

I felt that we should go to the hospital rather than sleep. I knew some things about first aid. The conditions in the hospital that night were the worst I've ever seen. My hands were filthy. They didn't have any kind of anesthetic. It was terrible! They'd just let the people yell and scream while they sewed up what they could. The floor was like butcher shop.

There was no time to clean up. There was nobody to clean up, really. I sewed up a few people. That's the first time I've ever done it. There were only two doctors in the hospital when we arrived. There were a few nurses. The only reason I started doing what I did was because one lady looked at what the others were doing and said, "Well, you can't do any worse," so I sewed a few people up.

The only thing they had to put on the wounds was streptomycin powder. There was no water so we just poured the powder into the wound. I said to my companion, "The people we treat tonight will have a chance. They might have infection, they might be treated under the dirtiest circumstances, but at least they're having the bleeding stopped." The showhouses had been filled to overflowing, and all those people . . . the ones that were still alive . . . were in the plaza just bleeding and waiting for morning when somebody could get in and carry them out. About 10:00 o'clock, the ambulance quit bringing people in. The doctors quit and tried to get some sleep and so did we. All that night there were tremors.

They started to bring in people at 6:00 o'clock (in the morning) and we left the hospital about 11:30 to go back to see the members. Even though we knew that they were all okay, we wanted to see where they were. We had left them as soon as we had found out that they were all right. The first thing we tried to do for the members that day after we left the hospital was to get them out and away from high walls and two-story buildings and things that might fall if there were another earthquake.

We'd visited all the member families that we knew the whereabouts of and told them to move out. We wanted to make a central location where we could have all the members camped where they could help each other and where, if we did get help, we could get it generally and they could all benefit. Without thinking, we'd moved them in with four other families right next to the hospital. Another cause for worry was that everyone that was sick would be right there at the hospital, too. We thought there might be a lot of typhoid; they were starting to give injections for typhoid that day. So we moved that family again from near the hospital to a little meadow about half a mile or a mile up in the hills near where we were staying. There they were away from people and where there was water that was being distributed. They'd bring it around in a big gasoline truck.

The next day I started giving typhoid shots. We set up a typhoid injection center. The Odar family, the owners of the tienda (store), had brought all their food and their clothing when they had moved out. They'd faired pretty well. They'd only had one grandmother killed, and their store had been left intact.

Elder Wilkins: The days kind of blur together. It seems like the (people) only think for right now. It was like a battle against our own people all the time. We'd say "You'd better get your vaccinations for typhoid," but they'd say, "We've heard that people are getting sick for a few hours from the shots. We don't want to get shots. We feel fine." And we'd say, "You'd better move out of your place." "Well, this is all we have, you know, and we can't move." We spent the first few days trying to get them settled with shots and a safe location.

Wednesday we decided we'd better go back to the church to see if we could get out the records and the money . . . (After lots of digging) We finally found the money and the records that day.

We were very dirty and very tired, and we still had on the suits that we'd put on to go to church Sunday morning. We really looked terrible, and felt worse. We went up the river past Los Pinos where we'd been staying, and found a little bit of privacy and took a bath in the river and changed our clothes.

When I first came to Lima they told me how cold that water up in the mountains was. They said, "Don't worry about the water in Lima . . . that's warm compared to the water in the mountains." But, wow! I've never felt any water that felt so good. It didn't matter if it were cold or hot or anything . . . it felt so good to be cleaned up again!

(Thursday) About 9:30 or so, some other men came into the hospital and said that they'd heard a voice down under the earth somewhere and they wanted some help to go get this little boy out. When we first got there, we heard his voice down under the ground and it was so faint. We decided we'd better stay and try to get him out even though it looked like it would be impossible.

We kept working and working and working. We didn't have shovels or picks or anything. All we had were our hands, and so it was quite slow. it was about 12:30, I guess, when we finally got this little boy out. I think the only thing that saved him was his will to live, because since 3:30 when it happened, he'd been in the same position . . . just trapped down there as if he had been poured in cement. We couldn't even see where he had been breathing from. He had been about six or eight feet under adobe bricks and dirt and rock, and he had not been able to move at all. We first ran into his hand. It was about an hour and a half after we found his hand before we could free him because we had to dig out around him just as if you were digging out dinosaur bones or something. When we got him out, he had a broken leg and his face was all puffed up and filled with dirt; but he was alive . . . We dug him out. He was lucky. There were a lot of people who were down there for a long time that died very slowly.

Elder Toone: I want to say that as I said at first, the reason we're here, I know, is because the Lord took care of us. If we had been in our house, even though it didn't fall down, we would have been killed because I'm sure that if we had been on the second story when we felt that earthquake, we wouldn't have been in the house very long. And if we had run out into the street, as narrow as those streets are in Huaraz, we would have been buried just like the Peace Corps girls . . . under two layers of adobe brick walls. If we had been in the church . . . and we had planned to be in our offices working that afternoon . . . there wouldn't have been a hope, as deeply buried as those offices later were. Even if we had run out of the chapel, the chapel street was the same way . . . buried under eight to ten feet of adobe bricks. Each adobe brick weighed more than forty pounds, so you can imagine what it would have been like. That we were giving a charla on the widest street in Huaraz where there were almost no buildings, at 3:00 o'clock on Sunday afternoon is a testimony that the Lord was watching over us.

Elder Wilkins: That's for sure, and I think having the members saved the way they were was another testimony. Almost everyone we talked to had dead in their families, some of the families had lost eight to ten people. Some parents had lost all of their children and we saw quite a few little children without homes. But every one of the members and investigators and their families were fine as far as we know. They lost their houses and things, but every one of them was fine. The Lord really did preserve them, even though a lot of them had been inactive for a long time. They were members and had been baptized and I'm sure the Lord really protected them. They knew it, too. We talked to many of them, and even the investigators bore their testimony that the Lord had really saved their lives.

Elder Toone: Yes. As we walked around the city after the earthquake, the thing that I noticed was that everyone seemed to have been caught doing just what they were usually doing on Sunday. The cinemas were full. It seemed like every other person was drunk. It was really something to hear everybody talk about the "desgracia." It was all over the hospital. Everybody felt that it was the Lord's displeasure with them.

THE RESCUE TEAM REPORTED THE FOLLOWING:

Elder Gillespie: We were getting higher, we could tell, because our lungs ached and we were just burning up inside. We spread two [blankets] on the ground and on top of us, and slept the width of it. With four of us on the blankets, they came to about our chins, and our feet stuck out. We finally hiked up to the punta. (About 14,000 feet)

Elder Newman: I remember looking back when Elder Gillespie was coming up over the point and seeing him faint on the trail. I remember seeing Elder Fales pull his boot off and his entire heel was a blister. There is a quality in great people that moves them to act upon situations. It's a quality that moves men to act upon situations, to face them fearlessly, to experience things that make men old and wise at the age of twenty or twenty-five; but it strengthens people and makes them grow, and I was proud to be a part of that company and proud to endure that experience with them, with those Elders.

Friday morning it took us from six o'clock until about 9:00 o'clock, I think, to get to the punta. It was another two or two-and-a-half hours from there to the city. Upon entering the city, we left our guide with his family and, wonderfully enough, they were all fine. He hadn't lost anyone in his family. The Lord blessed him in that.

Elder Fales: I was talking to a man about twenty-eight years old, who was a mountain climber from San Diego. After the earthquake, he was trying to find his own friends, and he'd hear people screaming under the piles of dirt. It was very hard for him to walk past them in order to find his friends and the people that he knew and to just leave the people there lying. He couldn't see them, but he could hear their screams for help. Also, he told me about a Peruvian girl he knew who was in a showhouse when it caved in. She was one of the few that were saved. The whole ceiling fell in and opened up in the middle. The roof fell and everybody all around her was killed and buried under it, but she stayed alive. She climbed out of the roof . . . Elder Gillespie and I -- I'm sure we all feel the same way -- were talking about how real the signs of the times are, and how much of an insight it gave to us as we talked about these real signs and how important it is that we take note of each sign we see. I don't think we should just throw them out as a kind of coincidence. I really learned to take note of these earthquakes, tremors, and falling stars we saw, and I realize that these are signs of the times. The scriptures talk about how in the last days there will be such commotion that the stars will cast themselves down. It was quite an experience seeing all those things.

Elder Gillespie: I think that the biggest problem was lack of organization. They might have quite a bit there, but it wasn't being distributed, as least not very effectively.

Elder Fairbanks: Another problem was trying to coordinate the different armed forces . . . the Peruvian with the American with the French, and, I believe, with even Japanese and the English. They weren't coordinated in any way. That's one of the things the Americans were complaining about. They weren't able to coordinate. Each was trying to do it on his own, and they couldn't get together and work together. It would have been much more effective if they had.

Elder Toone: The thing that I noticed most in the days after the earthquake, the thing that kept standing out, is that the people, after they got organized, dug things out of their houses. But the feeling that prevailed was they were just lost. They had lost their whole life. They dug things out of their houses . . . just a chair or a table, broken, and maybe a few pots and pans . . . something like that. I said, "Well, what are you going to do with these things?" They weren't worth anything. Everybody had loads and loads of junk, but nothing was worth anything. Of course, they'd realize it when you ask them; they'd say, "Well, I can't take that." "Well, what are you going to do with it?" They'd say, "Well, I'll sell it for whatever I can get out of it." Everyone was lost. They didn't know what they were going to do. They had lost their sense of values. They were trying to hold onto things that were, at one time, important to them; it was a sad situation. It's hard to describe the situation up there because, unless you have ever seen a city destroyed, it's impossible to tell you what it's like.

Elder Gillespie: The experiences of a lot of people in the town were so real, so tragic, that they couldn't accept it . . . we met a lady and said, "Well, hi, how are you, Hermana?" She said, "Oh, fine;" then she broke down and shed about three tears and said that her daughter had died. Later on, as we were going out of town, when we asked another fellow how he was, he said, "Oh, just great. I lost a sister, but that's all." There wasn't any mourning. They hadn't gotten a good hold of themselves. The situation didn't seem real to them.

Elder Fales: Great rocks had fallen off mountain cliffs and the road was all broken up. Right around the city of Huaraz some of the houses of the Indian people there weren't as broken up as a lot of the houses. For me it seemed that the innocent people around the city weren't hurt much, whereas right in the city itself, it seemed that there was a greater amount of destruction.

Elder Gillespie: Also, in regard to the number of people that were killed, I don't know how they counted them, but when we went to get on the bus, we walked into town a little bit and it still had the smell, meaning that there were probably many, many people who were still covered. They didn't clear the streets out; they just drove over the top. So you can imagine the number of people who had been in the street when the wall had fallen on them. I don't know if they'll ever find them.

Elder Fairbanks: Regarding rebuilding the city, the impression I got of the Peruvian people is that they are a patient people, that they don't really look into the future. And my opinion of Huaraz from what I saw up there and from talking to the people is that maybe the high class officials and the big businessmen will move out and they'll move down to Lima or one of the bigger cities where they can continue as such, while the lower class, the middle class, and the peasants, the farmers . . . they'll all stay there and they'll rebuild their homes little by little by little. In three or four years, I would imagine, some of the big businessmen will start moving back in again because their people will stay, and they'll redevelop business and they'll open transportation and things will start all over again, because they're just that kind of people. They just won't go anywhere. They say, "Well, I was born here. This is where I grew up." So they build their houses again. If there were another earthquake, I think the same thing would happen. It would just be a repeat of the same thing. The city will go on, and in a few more years it will be the same city that it was when it fell.

Elder Ladd Wilkins: Most streets are extremely narrow, and nearly all the buildings are made of adobe. As a result, nearly every building in the city fell, covering the streets and everyone in them. It was difficult for us to believe that such a catastrophe was actually happening. In our search for the members of the Church, we found many people seriously wounded or buried alive, but luckily we found eveyrone of the members alive and only a few with injuries. It really was a miracle, because as soon as we found out, there were only very few families without dead. One of the last estimates of the number of dead in Huaraz was 20,000, or 2 out of 5. We therefore felt extremely blessed in that none of our 50 members were killed.

It is hard to imagine that nature could cause all of this in only 2 minutes and 20 seconds. The whole city was weeping and mourning, and nearly everything was destroyed. Eight days after the earthquake hit, we found a way down to Lima. Although it was a 40 hour trip, we decided to leave.

While many were trying to deal with this tragedy in northern Peru, there were hundreds and thousands of missionaries and members in other parts of Peru and throughout the world who were quietly, but steadily, moving the work forward in their various fields of labor. They continued to obediently work, teach, serve and sacrifice. As they did, the stone spoken of by Daniel the prophet continued to roll forward to fill the earth.

Chapter 10

The Rosebud Begins To Blossom

June 14, 1970: The conference in Huanuco was held with good attendance. The first native Elders to be ordained in the Huanuco Branch were ordained tonight by President Litster. They were Juan Veliz and Eloy Bazan. (Eloy Bazan was later set apart as the first patriarch of the Huanuco Stake in 1990.)

August 1, 1970: This day the Andes Mission has officially been divided forming the Peru Mission and the Ecuador Mission.

December 31, 1970: At the close of the year there were 29 branches in the mission and five districts. Mission total . . . 8,119 members.

July 8, 1971: President and Sister Litster found that both have Infectious Hepatitis. They both had to be confined to bed for two to three weeks as a minimum.

July 17, 1971: President J. Robert Driggs, newly appointed President of the Andes Peru Mission, arrived in Lima.

July 28, 1972: This is the annual celebration of "Fiestas Patrias," the Peruvian Independence Day. All was quiet in the mission home. However, Sister Gomez of the Lima 2nd Ward departed early to present President Velasco, President of the Republic, with a specially prepared Book of Mormon. It was bound in leather and the cover had his name engraved in gold. It being Independence Day, the public was permitted to enter the Government Palace and shake the President's hand. Attempts had been made earlier to present the book to President Velasco but had failed. Sister Gomez prayed that the Lord would help her, and that it would be a sign of truthfulness unto her and that she would serve the Lord and His Church all her life if He would permit her to present the Book of Mormon to the President.

All people entering the palace were being searched, and all articles of every kind were being kept outside. As Sister Gomez neared the door, a guard recognized her (she worked in the government) and told her just to go on in. She entered and presented the Book of Mormon to President Velasco and said, "In behalf of all the members of the Church of Jesus Christ of Latter-day Saints, I present you this Book of Mormon, with the best of intentions. And, Mr President, I want you to know that all the Mormons pray for you and the progress of our country." He accepted the book and told her thank you.

November 5, 1972: The general session of the Lima Stake Conference. Elder Gordon B. Hinckley presented the name of Mario Perotti as president of the stake, with Robert Gibbons and Felipe Chavez as counselors. A record 1,188 people were in attendance.

August 5, 1973: An historic event took place in the "altiplano" when the first joint branch conference was held of the branches of Juliaca and Puno in the Juliaca Branch local. Over 100 members were in attendance and a great spirit was felt. President Jorge Rodriguez of the Juliaca Branch, who is leaving because of his work, was released as Branch President and was replaced by Elder Jerry Redd.

July 4, 1974: President and Sister Russell H. Bishop and family arrived in Lima this morning and were greeted by 100 missionaries and a great many members as they began their service in Peru.

December 21, 1974: This morning the mission leaders finished their business in Ayacucho by revisiting the

Ataurima family and talking with them. They found that they were the first family to be baptized that spoke only Quechua. That is the first family in this dispensation. The wife spoke nothing except Quechua and her husband translated the discussions for her.

From July 1966 *Improvement Era* (or Church News) it was reported that the first members of the Church taught in Quechua were baptised. They were sisters Antonia Ataurima and Virginia Espinoza and their husbands, Carlos Ataurima and Juan Espinoza. In December of 1967, Elder Douglas Earl was assigned to Ayacucho and in February of 1968 Ayacucho was closed for what would be about 11 years to missionaries. During a brief two month stay in Ayacucho, Douglas Earl was present at the birth of one of the Ataurima children, Roberto. He was also there when the branch was closed and the missionaries were removed. Twenty years later, in February of 1988 upon the organization of the Peru Lima East Mission, President Douglas Earl returned to Peru. Two of the first two missionaries assigned to him among the 112 missionaries were Jose Espinoza, son of Juan and Virginia Espinoza and Roberto Ataurima, son of Carlos and Antonia Ataurima. By then the parents spoke Spanish.

June 11, 1975: Five new Peruvian missionaries entered into their mission experience today. They are: Elder Juan Vergaray and Sister Ricardina Fores, both from the Chorrillos Ward, Lima, Peru Stake; Elders Oswaldo Carrion and Martin Gutierrez, both from the Lima 5th Ward, Lima Peru West Stake. These missionaries were interviewed by President Bishop and commenced their "Mission Home" experience. This was the first such experience in the history of the mission for Latin Missionaries. This special orientation covered two days in which rules, mission organization and missionary skills were discussed.

June 20, 1975: As a note of historical interest, on June 14, 1975, a 102-year-old woman was baptized in the Chimbote

1st Branch. Her baptism completed a family of 5 generations of "Mormons". Sister Emilia Cruz Valderrama is now the oldest known living member in the Peru Lima Mission. Despite her age she is still very active and helps with many of the daily household chores. Sister Cruz, the mother of 12 children, also has an adopted 11-year-old son who received the discussions and was baptized with her. The boy knows of no other mother besides his 102-year-old step-mother. From the first explanation of the Gospel presented by Elder Olsen and Elder Witt, Sister Cruz recognized the truthfulness of the message and showed keen interest in baptism.

October 21, 1975: At 9:00 p.m. a meeting was held with the district and ward and branch level officers of the Lima Peru Stake. The subject of the meeting was "Steps to get a Temple in Peru" and "Let's have group meetings to build membership."

January 15, 1976: Pucalpa is much like Iquitos. It is where the river joins the road to Lima so it is a real center of commerce. There are no paved streets in this very large town. But the people are the same, very friendly Lamanite people of the jungle. Pucalpa sits right on the Ucaylai river. There are many factories of all sorts and most of the men in town work in the factories. There are also many men that work in agriculture.

The people of the jungle have a very special custom. When someone is at their door, they invite them in and have them seated, and then ask what they can do for them and what they want.

Everyone in town during the rainy season has mud up to his ankles. It is just the way of life in Pucallpa. It was recommended that those elders that work in Pucallpa during the rainy season have a pair of boots to wear all day long (during the months of December, January, February, and March).

January 31, 1976:   Brother Modesto Palacios is a fine man and has been spreading "Mormonism" throughout the city. He is very well known in the community and is one of the Mayor's counselors. He also runs his own carpentry. He said that he has attended many of the churches only to find that they "estan un poco caidas" and looking for something. Brother Palacios has also taught in the school there and told us that with the new law passed of freedom of religious teaching, he would be interested in teaching the older jovenes about the gospel as a school subject.

The history continues: Juli has a very beautiful plaza and you can look down upon the shores of Lake Titicaca from the plaza. As the missionaries were looking again for a truck or other vehicle to take us to Ilave (in hope of finding transportation from there to Puno) we came upon a man who was reading his Bible. He introduced himself as Luis Chucuya, a father of 14 children. He said he was the Director of La Iglesia Evangelica Bautista de Jesus Nazarene. This church is probably one of the largest organized ones in Juli with about 60 members. We spoke with him of our church and left him a copy of the Book of Mormon, a few tracts, and our testimonies. He said that he felt we were sent from God and invited us to teach his congregation on Sunday. We left him and later passed by his house and he was busy reading his Book of Mormon with the Bible at his side.

October 5, 1976:   When Elders Mower and LeBaron arrived in Tarma, Elders Potter and Kupfur were not in their home, so Elders Mower and LeBaron went down to the plaza and talked to a lot of good men and took some good references. The other Elders were finally found eating in their pension. They had been out damming up a creek for the baptism that was held the next day.

October 6, 1976:   The Gave family was baptized bringing the number of members in Tarma to 7.

November 21, 1976: In the morning, Elder Bruce R. McConkie presided over the division of the Lima Peru West Stake. The results being the creation of the Lima Peru Central Stake and the Lima Peru Limatambo Stake. In the May 1977 issue of the *Ensign* magazine, Elder McConkie said, ". . . there are few things of which Israel's prophets have spoken with more fervor and zeal than the latter-day gathering of the house of Jacob and the part that favored people will play in the building of Zion again on earth . . . members of the church who live outside the United States and Canada would know why they are now counseled to remain in their own nations and not gather to an American Zion, I gave the following talk in the Lima Peru Area Conference . . . This gathering of Israel and this building of Zion in the last days occurs in stages . . . We are now engaged in gathering Israel within the various nations of the earth and in establishing stakes of Zion at the ends of the earth. This is the work that is now going forward in all of the nations of south America . . . (Ps. 102: 13, 16 & 18) . . . We have been called to preach the gospel to every nation kindred and tongue and people . . . Our call to men everywhere is, 'Come to Zion, come to Zion, and within her walls rejoice.' (*Hymns*, no.81) Now, what is Zion, and where shall she be established? . . . Zion is people: Zion is the saints of God; Zion is those who have been baptized; Zion is those who have received the Holy Ghost; Zion is those who keep the commandments; Zion is the righteous; or in other words, as our revelation recites: 'This is Zion - the pure in heart." (D&C 97:21) . . . In the language of the Book of Mormon, it (the gathering of israel) consists of being 'restored to the true church and fold of god,' and then 'gathered' and 'established' in various 'lands of promse.' (2 Ne. 9:2) . . . Zion is the pure in heart; we gain purity of heart by baptism and by by obedience. A stake is like founding a City of Holiness. Every stake on earth is the gathering place for the lost sheep of Israel who live in its area. The gathering place for Peruvians is in the stakes of Zion in Peru, or in the places which soon will become stakes . . ." (pp. 115-118)

January 1, 1977: The Peru Mission was officially divided today to form the Peru Lima North and Peru Lima South Missions. Total number of baptisms for the year of 1976 was 1708.

February 25, 1977: In the morning President Spencer W. Kimball, accompanied by his second counselor, Marion G. Romney, Elder Bruce R. McConkie and L. Tom Perry, of the Council of the Twelve, President A. Theodore Tuttle of the First Quorum of the Seventy, and Elder Robert D. Hales of the First Quorum of the Seventy, arrived in Lima, Peru. They were accompanied by their respective wives and a large number of other members of the official Area Conference entourage.

Early Friday afternoon, a meeting was held with U. S. Embassy personnel, Stake President Perrotti, President Vidal, President Bishop and Brother Kennedy. During this meeting the problem of missionary visas was considered. It was felt that a meeting should be arranged with the Minister of Foreign Affairs and the Minister of Internal Affairs during the return visit of Brother Kennedy to Lima on the 4th of March. At 3:30 a press conference was held in the Conference Room of the Crillon Hotel, during which conference President Spencer W. Kimball addressed the members of the press and those present and explained the basic reasons for the existence of the Church. A very beautiful and concise explanation was presented concerning the Book of Mormon, the message of Restoration, the First Vision and the early days of Church. Many questions were asked by the members of the press, all of which were answered in a most orderly and precise manner by President Kimball, President Romney and Brother Kennedy.

At 4:30, a very lovely banquet was presented in the Sheraton Hotel. All of the above mentioned members were present along with the Stake Presidents, their Counselors, Mission Presidents and their Counselors, and accompanied by their wives. In addition to these leaders of the Lima area, the District Presidencies from the eight districts in Peru along with their wives were also in attendance. Patriarch Jose Santos Ojeda and his wife were also present at the banquet. President Bishop gave a welcome to all present. The meeting was opened by a prayer offered by President Romulo Casos, first counselor in the Peru Lima South Mission. After the first course, all members present were introduced to the Prophet by President Bishop.

Following the banquet, the official party, preceded by a police escort, left from the Sheraton Hotel to the Amauta Theater (Gran Teatro Amauta) where a large crowd of approximately 12,000 to 13,000 people enthusiastically greeted the Prophet and those of the official party. This gathering was the first session of the conference and was officially opened by President Russell H. Bishop who gave a welcoming comment to all present. This meeting was opened by prayer offered by President Jose Sousa.

The cultural program was hosted and directed by Freddy Fernandez and Eliana Montano. The program consisted of many fine entertaining numbers of song and dance and dramatization from the stakes of Lima and the branches from the provinces. Following the meeting at the Amauta, a large enthusiastic group was on hand to greet the prophet as he and the official party returned to the hotel.

February 26, 1977: Second day of the Area Conference. At 9:30 a.m. the police escorted bus, with the official party, departed for the Amauta Theater. At 10:00 a.m. the General Session commenced. A very heart-warming initial address was given by President Kimball, followed by addresses from President Tuttle and Elder Perry and other local authorities of the Church. The session continued until 12:00 noon at which time the party went to the Tambo de Oro restaurant for a buffet luncheon. Following the luncheon, a brief bus tour of Lima, including the Inquisition Museum and the Gold Museum, was taken by the official party members.

At 7:00 p.m. two sessions of the Conference were held. One session for the mothers and daughters and female members was conducted in the Limatambo chapel. The Chapel had been renovated with walls and ceilings having been painted and all benches being refinished. The overflow crowd was seated in the parking lot next to the Limatambo chapel. The Priesthood Session was conducted in the Amauta Theater. The main speakers during this session were President Romney and Elder McConkie. The session ended at 9:00 p.m.

February 27, 1977: The last day of the Conference was similar to the Saturday sessions, commencing at 10:00 and ending at 12:00. An additional meeting was held for the missionaries in the two missions with Elder McConkie, President Tuttle, and Elder Hales, accompanied by Dr. Wilkinson, all of whom spoke to the missionaries. The meeting was conducted by President Jose Armando Sousa.

The last General Session commenced at 7:00 p.m. and concluded at 9:00. The party returned to their hotel around 9:30 p.m.

May 1, 1977: During a work visit in Cuzco on May 1st (a fast Sunday), the missionaries picked up investigators in the morning to take to church. About 20 people in total were present and it was very enjoyable. Most were investigators with much interest and that were to be baptized soon.

That night, with a decision of whom to visit, Elder Estrada thought for a moment and then decided to visit one family (another Mamanis family):

When we arrived they said that they had been waiting for us. We finished the discussion on "The Plan of Salvation" with them. Then we looked at each other asking whether we should challenge or not. We decided yes and began to talk for a while about all the teachings they had received. Then we arrived at the question of "When you

know that these things are true you will want to what?" ...
They said "Follow them." We then pulled out 3 Nephi 31:10-11 and explained how they could follow them.

We then recommended that they prepare themselves for the fourteenth of May for their baptism and asked for a show of hands for those that accepted. First all the kids raised their hands to be baptized. After looking around and feeling uncomfortable with his hand down, Dad raised his and finally seeing that all of her family was going to be baptized, Mom didn't want to be left out so raised her hand also.

We then went through the lacing process and obtained 5 families to invite to their baptism. Afterwards they were very excited about their baptism, not to mention the excitement of the elders. It was a great charla and Elder Estrada did a fine job in it. We ended with a prayer kneeling on their dirt floor. At the end the father stood up with tears in his eyes and we all left with a great spirit.

Chapter 11

A Time of Re-Dedication

<u>June 26, 1977</u>: The Ilo Branch was created in Ilo, Department of Moquegua. Those present were President Romula Casos Bellido and President Francisco N. Davila C. Brother Guillermo Schawrz was called as Branch President.

<u>June 28, 1977</u>: President Norval C. Jesperson arrived in the mission field accompanied by his wife, Sybil, his daughter, Jill, and his son, Spencer. They arrived at the Jorge Chavez airport at 10:00 a.m. They were greeted at the airport by the Bishops and by all of the missionaries that were working in the Lima area at the time. Also present were a number of friends and Priesthood leaders from the Lima area. A luncheon was held in the mission home after their arrival and then they commenced the orientation of President Jesperson.

Elder David Thorne recorded the following incident which took place while he was serving in Huancayo:

<u>July 11, 1977</u>: We heard rumors that there might be problems today and that the university students were going to protest. Before we came home we bought some food to tide us over. I can still hear the gun shots and people running in the streets.

<u>July 12, 1977</u>: Before we went out this morning, my companion and I had prayer and asked the Lord to bless and protect us and he did exactly that because right after we got home, Elder Maestre came running in our room and told us that Elder Perez and Elder Uceda had been shot and wounded near the main square at about 9:30 a.m. We had walked by that same square at 10:30 a.m. Elders Perez and Uceda had been

shot all over their bodies with buckshot and the force of the shot had knocked them to the ground. A man walking behind them got a bullet in the leg. Elder Maestre, who also was walking with them, received a few pellets also. After they had been knocked down by the shots they got up and ran to a police clinic about three blocks above the plaza.

<u>July 16, 1977</u>: Elders Uceda and Perez were in pretty bad shape. When I saw them they were in bed lying on their stomachs because their backs and legs were covered with buckshot and they were in pain. From what I have gathered, the people in the streets started to yell and whistle at the car and the white shirts of the Elders must have attracted the attention of the police and they started shooting at them. Elder Maestre saw this coming and hit the ground and was only grazed by a few pellets. From his fall, however, Elder Maestre reinjured his wound from his appendix operation he had a couple of weeks ago. Elders Uceda and Perez weren't quite so lucky and got hit by a shower of pellets. They did manage to cover their faces and turn their backs. They were knocked down by the shots but they got up and ran to safety. A man they were walking with got shot by a bullet in his leg. The wounded Elders then went to the Police Clinic where they took out the majority of the pellets. The police wanted them to stay there for a few days but the Elders thought it best to leave. The Elders left and went to the Wu's hotel for treatment. President Jesperson and Elder Parmenter had landed in Jauja at about 3:30 p.m. but when they landed, there were about twenty soldiers on the airstrip with machine guns awaiting them They had safe conducts to Huancayo but the soldiers said it wasn't safe and that they had to leave Jauja. They flew to the nearest airstrip in San Ramon and called us from there. On the phone they told us that they would be staying the night in San Ramon and that we should all stay the night in the hotel and that the next morning we should meet them in the airport at Jauja at 7:00 a.m. Fortunately there were some men staying in the hotel that night who were leaving that next morning at 6:00 a.m. passing through Jauja on their way to Ayacucho who said

they would take us. I will never forget the ride from Huancayo to Jauja. On the road there were rocks, fallen trees, tree stumps, and any other thing you could think of. When we rounded the final bend and could finally see the airport my companion said, "There's the airplane." We loaded up in the ten man, two -engined airplane and took off. It was a forty-five minute plane ride to Lima. Finally on July 20 we returned to Huancayo and things were about back to normal.

The mission history recorded the incident as follows:

<u>July 14, 1977:</u> We received news that 2 of our Elders, Carlos Uceda and Percy Perez, had been seriously wounded in Huancayo by shotgun fire and were in need of medical aid. This really was a shock to us and we decided to go as quickly as possible to their aid. We called Elder Gene R. Cook in Quito, Ecuador, and he advised us that it was at our discretion to use a small commercial airline known as Sassa to fly up and fly the wounded Elders out. It was also suggested that we fly out the other Elders while we were there since the disturbances in Huancayo were of such a severe nature that it appeared that there might be a curfew imposed which would cut off all activities after 5:00 p.m. for a long period of time. There also seemed to be danger to the other missionaries as there was a lot of gunfire heard in the city. Elder Parmenter and the President flew up that afternoon and landed in the city of Juaja, a city close to Huancayo high in the Andes Mountains at about 10,000 feet. We were then met at the airport by armed troops who told us that we had no permission to stay and that we could not go into Huancayo to take the missionaries out in spite of the fact that they were wounded and needed urgent medical care. We did, at Elder Cook's suggestion, get a letter from the American Embassy introducing us as Americans who needed to evacuate American Nationals from the area but that still didn't seem to do much good. However, after reading the letter and hearing our pleas, the Lieutenant in charge of the troops at the airport did, in fact, soften his attitude and pleaded with his captain to allow us to extract the wounded Elders and

the Americans, but to no avail. We then had to proceed on to the city of San Ramon which is a jungle city about 20 minutes by air by about 6 hours in car from Juaja. We spent the night there in San Ramon.

<u>July 15, 1977:</u> In the morning hours, we returned to Juaja and were able to evacuate the missionaries from Huancayo. While in San Ramon, we were able to see for the first time the cities of San Ramon and La Merced which appear to be ripe areas for missionary work, in fact, the hand of the Lord could have been leading us to those areas in order to open them up for the missionary effort at some later date. When we did return to Juaja, the troops had left the airport and we were able to land. The authorities also had relented and their hearts had softened; I am sure this was because of the prayers of the Elders in Huancayo. The missionaries had been given safe conduct to leave Huancayo and return with us to Lima. We took all of the missionaries out of Huancayo, including the sisters and returned them to Lima this same day. When we returned, there were newspaper reporters and television photographers in great numbers surrounding us attempting to extract from us the story of the occurrences but we remained almost completely silent.

When President and Sister Jesperson returned to the airport some time later, a man recognized President Jesperson and asked, "Aren't you the man who flew out with the missionaries?" When he acknowledged that he was the same person, the man told him that 5 minutes after they flew out of the airport with the missionaries from Huancayo, the soldiers came with orders to kill everyone. . .Sister Jesperson said the plane was so loaded down that it hardly got off the ground and when they returned to Lima, President Jesperson met their first group of North American Missionaries in jeans and an old sweater. That's how they started their mission.

<u>July 26, 1977:</u> Elder Gene R. Cook arrived at the airport in the morning with his wife on Branniff Airlines where

we received them. They were met at the airport by President and Sister Jesperson. Elder Cook then spent the rest of the day with President Sousa in the North Mission, then came the following morning to spend the day with President Jesperson, instructing him with regard to several important programs: namely the program of judging ourselves by new standards (i.e., number of baptisms, number of people committed to baptism, number of discussions taught, discussions taught with members, and the number of investigators brought to church.) Also, the concept of the quality of the baptisms that we are having: (i.e., number of adults baptized, number of adult males over 21 and over 18 years of age, and the number of families baptized) such being good indicators of quality missionary work. He also gave excellent instruction on how to get member involvement in the missionary activity. The entire day was spent going over problems with Elder Cook to the great benefit of President Jesperson and, I am sure, to the advantage of the Peru Lima South Mission.

September 2-3, 1977: President Jesperson and his assistants went to Cuzco to effect a reorganization of the Quechua program. The Elders in the Quechua Program met with the President and the Assistants for an all-day meeting in one of the chapels in Cuzco, at which time the program was completely revised. The missionaries were brought into Cuzco from all the small villages in the mountains. Since Cuzco itself is heavily populated with Lamanite people, it was felt that the missionairies could be more effective there than in the villages. In four and one half months, there had been a total of only three converts in the Quechua Program there.

The plan now is to have the plan develop for the next several months, keeping the largest numbers of missionaries in Cuzco, and as the program grows, to gradually expand their activities into the surrounding cities and large towns. Sending missionaries far out into the mountains will be avoided for at least several years, until the cities of most of the population have been adequately covered.

October 20, 1977: President and Sister Jesperson, Brother Bohman and Brother Davis flew to Cuzco. During the flight, President Jesperson sat across from a man who was a religious leader a group of religious zealots who met three times a year in a small village an hour's drive from Cuzco. This man invited President Jesperson to come and address the group of approximately four hundred people for an entire afternoon. President Jesperson, thinking this would be a glorious opportunity to preach the Gospel, agreed. Upon arriving in Cuzco, President and Sister Jesperson, Eb Davis, Fred Bohman and four missionaries went on a four-hour drive by taxi to a small village near Cuzco and preached to about three hundred people. Some of the Elders stationed in Cuzco spoke Quechua and addressed the group in that language. Some of the Elders returned the 21st and took many referrals. This was possibly the first time that the Gospel had been preached to that large group of Indians in Peru.

The branch in Toquepala became an ensign to the nation. With the help of that little group, a district that included Tacna, Toquepala, and Arica, Chile, the first district in Peru, was organized with Marion Robinson as President, as was the first Quorum of Elders (Marvin Brown as President). Both these men from Toquepala have since served as Mission Presidents. Districts were then organized in Lima, in the north (combining Piura, Chiclayo and Trujillo), and in Arequipa.

The rise and fall of the church in Toquepala was related to the principle of fasting that when leadership was plentiful the branch operated well with good attendance and high activity. As Peruvian mine workers were baptized they apparently suffered persecution and harassment from their colleagues. It also seems that perhaps one of the common tendencies was to be baptized into the church for the simple reason that the directors of the mine were Mormons. The church continued this way until one day there was an exchange of words between one of the North American members and a Peruvian official, which initiated an investigation and the final expulsion of several of the church leaders and a restriction on the number of North American families that would be permitted to be employed in Toquepala. After this and the departure of several of the North American families who were leaders in the Branch; the chapel was bought by the company and the body of the church was left without organization and leadership. This situation has continued until the present time when there are no organized meetings, no church authority or set apart leadership, and limited contact between members.

January 6, 1978: Elder Packer, Elder Gene R. Cook, and Brother Eb Davis of the Indian Translation Service for the Church, will travel to Cuzco to look at the Quechua Program as well as the need for new missionaries in Peru. The Church is emphasizing the need for Peruvian missionaries to support themselves during their missions.

January 21, 1978: President and Sister Jesperson flew to Cuzco. From Cuzco, they went by taxi to Urabamba to meet Elders Figueroa and Turley who arrived three weeks earlier to open the work there which constitutes the full opening of the work with the Quechua speaking people. Elders Thomas S. Monson and Gene R. Cook accompanied the Jespersons on their trip.

May 8, 1978: President Jesperson received a call from Elder Gene R. Cook in which he was told that the Peru Arequipa Mission had been approved by the First Presidency and that it would be organized beginning July 1st. He would head the new Peru Arequipa Mission and President Milton Wille, the Peru Lima South Mission.

October 31, 1978: The Sao Paulo Temple played a role in the development of the Church in Peru. We left Lima Tuesday, October 31, at 9:30 p.m. While we were at the airport waiting for our flight we met two families from Ecuador that were on their way to Sao Paulo to attend the temple. It was so exciting to see members of the Church that were able to make this long trip to go to the temple. The one family was an Indian family from back in the mountains. They were dressed in the typical Ecuadorian Indian dress. The mother and two small daughters, about 4 and 11 years old, were dressed in long dark skirts and a dark shawl type garment they had tied around their shoulders and a turban on their heads that hung way down their backs. They wore multiple strings of gold-colored beads around their neck that formed a collar about eight inches wide and bands of tiny beads around their wrists about four inches wide. The father and one teenage son wore white pants, dark felt hats and dark colored ponchos that they folded very precisely back over their shoulders. We visited with them quite a while and the father, Rafael Tobango, said that he is the district president up in his area, that the three children they had with them were three of four living and that they had 11 deceased children. The father told me that he had had many dreams and visions about the Church. Sister Mitchel, wife of the Equador-Guayaquil Mission President, said that he told them that Moroni came and taught him how to read and write. She says that he didn't know how before and that now he does, so someone taught him how. (I cannot verify this as being true.) She also said that they were very poor, but sold some land in order to go to the temple in Sao Paulo. They were very interesting.

Wednesday afternoon we went over to the temple. The dedication was beautiful. When Elder Hinckley spoke on Thursday, he said that about ten years ago he had visited Brazil and had felt so bad as he visited a family who had Negro ancestry. The parents were both active in the Church, the mother was the Relief Society president and they were all faithful in their Church activities. He said as he returned to his hotel room he pled with the Lord, asking why such faithful members of the Church should be denied the blessings of the Priesthood and he seemed to hear the answer that they had not yet been tried sufficiently. Then came the building of the temple and those members of the Church of Negro ancestry contributed their time, their money and their talents with no reservations -- knowing all the time that they would not be able to participate in the temple blessings. And then the Father said, "It is enough," and the blessings of the Priesthood were extended to all worthy male members of the Church. He then went on to say that as he sat in the dedication service on Wednesday afternoon there was a black man sitting on the fifth row with his arm around his little daughter sitting next to him. His wife and older daughter were singing in the choir and as the dedication prayer ended he looked up through tears to see the tears streaming down the strong, dark cheeks of that man. He turned and looked at the wife as tears streamed down her face as they say "The Hosanna Anthem." When President Kimball talked he also spoke of the new revelation. He said he had spent hours in humble prayer concerning this point. He told the Lord he had always supported and sustained the Church in its stand concerning the blacks and that he would support and sustain it as long as he lived if that was what the Lord wanted. And then he said, it was made known to him that the Lord wanted the blacks to have the Priesthood. He said all of the General Authorities and all of the membership of the Church had expressed their approval and sustaining vote. He indicated that the world as a whole had been happy to hear of the new policy except for a few "soreheads." His translator had a bit of a problem on that one and asked him what he had said and President Kimball turned to him and repeated "soreheads" with a little emphasis. All the gringos got a kick out of that. Both sessions that we attended were outstanding.

After the dedication we were taken on a tour of the temple. It is just beautiful. I think they said it is the smallest of all the temples with only two endowment rooms and no chapel or waiting room, but it is just beautiful. The furniture was made by a local member and is elegant. The temple president's wife, a sister to our neighbor Helen Jonsson, told us of many of the experiences they had getting the temple ready. She indicated that it is a great series of miracles. She said that members of the Church cleaned the temple from top to bottom after it was opened for public viewing and before the dedication. She said the women took down every little crystal from the chandeliers and polished them -- many with tears in their eyes. Some from joy and others because of the fact that once it was dedicated they would not be able to come back because of non-member or inactive husbands. She said Brazil doesn't let you import things, but when they went down they took a large box of sacred things to be used in the temple and the customs didn't touch anything. They were having a hard time getting the materials for the sacred clothing and one day one of the brethren came to Paulson's apartment and said, "The adversary just doesn't want us to have the sacred clothing we need and the temple cannot function without the clothing. Would you like to join us in a fast to help get the materials we need?" Green material that they had been able to get was yellowish in spots and the embroidery machines would not sew on it. After their fast they went to four places to find material and three of the four places referred them to the same place. She said this is unheard of in Brazil. The competition is so great that no one refers anyone to someone else. So they were able to get the beautiful green material that worked fine on the machines. It was perfect throughout the whole bolt with no yellow spots. Then the woman who was embroidering the aprons broke her arms and was unable to work for a month, but in spite of it all, everything was done on time and everything was beautiful. Also training the temple workers was a miracle. They had just three weeks to teach them everything before the temple opened for ordinance work and many of the temple workers had not yet had the privilege of going through the temple. Before it was opened for ordinance work to the general membership they took temple workers through in the evenings after the dedication services. There was certainly a sweet spirit there of gratitude, love and sacrifice.

We feel so grateful and so blessed for the privilege of having these wonderful experiences. It makes us feel even more the urgency of preparing the people of Peru to receive the blessings of a temple and ultimately to have a temple here in Peru for the people on the west side of South America.

Because of their poverty, the temple is still out of reach of most of our people. Only two women from Peru were able to attend the temple dedication and stay to do their temple work.

January 11, 1979: On a mountain overlooking Lima, Peru, members of the church along with the missionaries, Peruvian government leaders and press were together for the Dedicatory Services for the land of Peru. This special meeting was presided over by President Ezra Taft Benson, with Elder Roberto Vidal (Regional Representative) conducting. They began by singing an opening hymn, "High on a Mountain Top," after which President Jose Sousa (Peru Lima North Mission) and Elder Gene R. Cook (Andes Area Supervisor) offered brief remarks. A special number, "I Know that My Redeemer Lives," was sung. Remarks and a Dedicatory Prayer was given by President Benson. This meeting was concluded by singing "The Spirit of God Like a Fire is Burning."The Savior said it was the same whether He spoke or His servants spoke. This would apply equally to whether the servant acting for Him whether he was an Apostle or an Elder.

When the La Merced Branch was organized on November 21, 1981, the following Dedicatory Prayer was offered by Elder Craig Bushman, one of the full-time missionaries serving in Peru:

> Our Beloved Father in Heaven, in the name of they Beloved Son, Jesus Christ, our Savior and Redeemer, we, thy missionaries, the leaders and members of the Church, come before thee and kneel before thy throne on this special occasion to thank you for the many blessings we receive at thy hand.
>
> We thank thee, Father, for the beautiful creations, for this beautiful city of La Merced, for the marvels that thy hands have made in this world.

We thank thee, Father, for the opportunity to share the Gospel of Jesus Christ with our brothers here and for the blessings of the fulness of the Gospel.

We thank thee, Father, for the leaders of the church, especially for a living Prophet, for the guidance and direction that we receive through him, for President Groberg and the local leaders in La Merced.

We thank thee for the people here in La Merced and for their desires to hear the gospel and for the blessing of sharing it in their homes.

We also thank thee, Father, for the example of the members of the Church here, as a light to all those of La Merced.

We thank thee for the protection we receive at thy hand and for the health we enjoy, for the wisdom and promises we receive through our obedience, for the commandments and counsel to live our lives better and happier. Especially, we wish to thank thee for the restoration of the Gospel in its fullness in these times when we with our children are guided in righteousness through the example of Jesus Christ and his teachings.

We thank thee, Father, for our weaknesses and challenges, that we may perfect ourselves and progress to become more like thee through faithfulness and righteousness.

We wish to thank thee for the restoration of thy Holy Priesthood through thy servants Peter, James and John, who restored the Priesthood to Joseph Smith, thy servant and Prophet, that we may have the blessings of baptizing and doing ordinances in thy name and with authority.

We thank thee for this beautiful day and for the opportunity to express to thee the desires of our hearts in humility, for the knowledge that thou are our Beloved Father in Heaven, who hears and answers our prayers.

We come to thee, Father, this morning with a special purpose. Having been a custom in thy Church to dedicate all places in their due time, we are gathered with the leaders of thy Church in La Merced in our desire to dedicate this beautiful city and its surrounding areas to the preaching of the Restored Gospel.

We ask thee, Father, to soften the hearts of thy children in this city that they may be more receptive to the Holy Ghost.

As missionaries, we ask thee to help us to remember the responsibilities we have as ambassadors and to remember at all times and in all places that we are special witnesses of thy Son. Help us to fulfill the mission rules. We ask thee to bless the missionaries with the ability to present the Gospel so as to touch the hearts of thy children in La Merced. We ask thee to bless us that we may always seek thy Spirit and never receive too much knowledge to cause us to forget our dependence on thee. We ask thee to bless us with the ability to overcome all obstacles that the adversary may place in our path and with determination to serve thee to the end. We ask thee to help us to remember that this is not our time, but thine and that through obedience, we may be successful in our missions.

We ask thee to allow thy Spirit to descend upon this region, that the people may enjoy the blessings that the Gospel may bring them.

Now, our Beloved Father in Heaven, we make known to thee the desires of the leaders of the branch in La Merced. They desire strength to be generous, affectionate and dedicated to the missionary work in the city of La Merced. All this that thou mightest bless them abundantly with thy Spirit and open the hearts of our brethren who live in spiritual darkness and that thou mightest bless them with knowledge that they may work in righteousness. They know that through missionary work they are showing that they love thee above all other things. They know that they are lights that brighten the faith of others in Jesus Christ. Through their faith have greater love for each other with joy and happiness in Jesus Christ.

Father, we are grateful for the many blessings we receive at thy hand. In the name of thy Beloved Son, Jesus Christ, and by the power of the holy Priesthood of thy Son, we dedicate this city and the surrounding areas officially and particularly for the preaching of the Restored Gospel of thy Son. We dedicate also unto thee, our lives, talents and abilities that thou hast given us, all that we are, that we may bring to pass thy great and marvelous work. We ask thee, Father, to bless us that we may touch the hearts of thy children here and show them thy great power and love, that thy name and the name of thy Son may be glorified.

These things we ask thee in the name of Jesus Christ, Amen.

On April 8, 1984, the Church News reported that:

> Nearly 11,000 members of the Church attended a nine-stake conference here March 24 - 25 -- believed to be the largest gathering ever of members in Peru. They met in Amauta Coliseum in east Lima. They noted that Peru is the leading country in the world in convert baptisms. Missionaries are now baptizing about 1,000 converts each month.

The Church in Peru has grown to more than 70,000 members in 16 stakes since the first missionaries came in 1957.

In a priesthood meeting March 24, Elder Perry addressed some 1,200 leaders. "The Church here will never be the same after this meeting," he declared. He outlined the duties of leaders and explained the need to seek out inactive members. He also emphasized the importance of preparing for the temple now being built in Lima.

Jose Sousa, regional representative, commented after the conference that the Church has grown significantly stronger in Peru during the past few years. "Seeing the 10,800 members meeting together to hear the word of the Lord causes me to think that the rose is already blossoming in the desert."

Chapter 12

Recent History

President Joseph Groberg was invited by Elder Angel Abrea to share the following example of what was happening in this beloved land:

"Today, May 10, 1984, I set apart Elder O. . . ., the first missionary to be called from the . . . Branch. Sunday, May 6, 1984, he stood in his own fast and testimony meeting and expressed the desire he had secretly held: to begin a mission a mission the very day he could -- twelve months after his baptism. In a timely manner, his interviews were completed. His papers were in. He wondered why his call had not arrived. Three days later (yesterday), on the day of his anniversary, May 9, 1984, an unsuspecting traveler arrived with mail, among which was a letter for the branch president. It was the mission call. It read: "You should be in Lima, ready to serve, on May 9, 1984." What grateful joy spread across their faces as both president and Elder read and reread the call. But the day was half gone and there was perhaps too much to do.

Lima, the City of Kings, the capital, though only 225 kilometers from the mountain village, lay across untraveled roads, 15,000 feet below, on the coast -- a world, a universe away. They parted: one to gather funds, the other to pack what things he owned: a shirt, a tie, the books he would use. All fit in a single case. Soon the president arrived at the Elder's cottage with what he had collected from the saints going from door to door: 5,000 soles here, 10,000 there, and from his own precious reserve, a treasured ten dollar bill. The entire branch turned out with support and blessings, smiles and waves goodbye as Elder O., their first missionary, rose above the city on the winding path towards Lima. For a moment he paused, turned and smiled at his blue and lovely mountain home, the village of his birth, then, with uplifted hand sweeping across the sky, saluting those who watched proudly from below, he turned again and marked on to the appointed place and time.

President Groberg concluded, "Our experiences were unique and special, but no more unique nor special than all of those of all the missionaries and mission president before, during, and after our time. We all had the blessing of being in the Lord's work at a special time, in a special place, and among a special people."

President Dale Christensen learned that we are all called to serve. "We are all missionaries and we all have investigators to teach. Our wives and husbands and our children are our most important investigators. We need to teach the Gospel to them in our homes, and we need to teach it by the spirit and power of the Holy Ghost.

"We are all preparing to serve missions in the future. Some of us are preparing for our first mission at 19 years of age. Others for "missions" with our spouse after we retire. All of us are preparing for a mission to the spirit world to preach the Gospel to the spirits of those who did not have the opportunity to hear it in this life. We all can move the work forward now by preparing ourselves and our children and by contributing our resources as we have been invited and commanded to do.

'Even the little children can be missionaries. They are such great missionaries to us and to others and can pierce the hearts of many with their simple faith and pure testimonies. Our children were always eager to share a pamphlet with a stranger and tell someone about the church. They became quite involved and caught up in the mission and in living in Peru. They wanted to visit all the sights and ancient ruins. They became quite the archeologists.

"Once while hosting President and Sister James Young, a new mission president and his family, we visited the ancient ruins of Pachacamac just 20 minutes south of Lima. Of course, we were talking about the Book of Mormon and the Nephites and Lamanites as we pulled over to park and begin our walk. Immediately, the door to the van came open and the children jumped out and began to dig in the sand. As I walked around the front of the van, Jonathan stood there holding up his first important discovery. With excitement, he held up an old, broken and warped 45 rpm record and said, "Look what I found Dad!" Teresa Joy then shouted, "Look Dad, Jonathan found an ancient record!"

"Just then Samuel came running over holding an old piece of broken bathroom tile and said, "Ya, but I found one of the glass plates!" Isn't it wonderful, we always find just what we are looking for.

"On one of our first trips to Tarma, high in the Andes Mountains, I met a young man as I was walking out of the hotel on our way to attend our evening leadership meetings. We visited for a few moments, and I gave him my card and a personal invitation to visit our new chapel and attend services. He knew nothing of the church, but he knew where the chapel was in the middle of town.

"A month later, we returned to Tarma and were met at the chapel by the zone leaders who immediately introduced us to one of their new contacts. Elder King told me I had invited him to come to church a month earlier. I then remembered the encounter, but did not recognize him as it had been dark the night we spoke in front of the hotel.

"I asked him if the missionaries had taught him. He said, "Yes". I then asked him what he thought of their message. He responded, "I have gained a testimony and I was baptized last night". We were all thrilled.

"Probably one of the best missionary discussions ever given in Peru was taught one Sunday afternoon on our way home from a conference in Huanuco. I call it "Sacando su burro del barro en el dia de reposo". In English that means, "Pulling your donkey out of the mire on the Sabbath Day".

"Soon after leaving the city, we came upon a long line of traffic backed up from the night before because of a "Huayco" (pronounced "wyko") or avalanche that had covered the road. Sometimes a Huayco was caused by the whole mountain side sliding down over the road. Other times it was just mud or water. This time it was a mud slide about two feet deep with a line of over 50 buses full of people on both sides. They had been waiting for many hours and some for the whole night. It was Sunday and there were no bulldozers to help. A large bus and a small Toyota pickup had tried to cross and both were stuck in the middle. The bus finally got out, but the pickup couldn't move. They had been there for hours.

"There were more than 300 people on both sides of the road watching the driver try to dig the boulders out from in front of the wheels, but no one was helping him. Immediately, both Elder Jeff Peterson and Elder Tim Shields decided to go forward and help this man and get things moving. They rolled up their shirt sleeves and waded into the mud that was knee deep. Almost in chorus the spectators began to chide them and jeer at these two tall blond gringos in white shirts and ties. They hissed and booed and told the "Mormons" to go home. They even threw rocks at them.

"The Elders just smiled, ignored the rest and went to work. A silent hush came over the crowd as they dug out one boulder after another. With one great heave, they almost freed the vehicle. By this time the crowd began to believe that maybe they could get the job done. The whole feeling of the group changed from criticism to encouraging comments and compliments. Just then a drunk heckler stepped forward and threw a large boulder about the size of a grapefruit which landed just a foot from Elder Shields splashing mud all over him. As the heckler shouted some profanities and was attempting to throw another stone, four or five men grabbed him roughed him up a big for having potentially slowed things down. It was almost comical.

"After a lot of work, with a final show of strength, the two Elders literally lifted the back of the pickup out of the mud and over the last few boulders. As they pushed, the back wheels were spinning and throwing mud all over them. As the truck fish-tailed out, they jumped aboard and rode out of there like champions with cheers and shouts from everyone. Everyone then ran back to their buses and cars to continue their journey.

"We had passed many of the buses as we traveled and had stopped to wash the mud out of our clothes in the river by the highway. As each bus passed by, they waved and cheered and thanked us. I am certain that every person who witnessed that event was much more receptive when the missionaries knocked on their doors because of the example of these two missionaries and the service they gave.

"The Gospel is like that. Unless we get in and work, no one can progress. How beautiful were these two handsome missionaries who were covered from head to foot with mud and who had won the hearts of hundreds of people that day. As Isaiah said,

> How beautiful upon the mountains are the feet of him that bringeth good tidings, that publisheth peace; that bringeth good tidings of good,that publisheth salvation; that saith unto Zion: Thy God reigneth! (Isaiah 52:7)

Elder F. Burton Howard once said that he thought that "Isaiah might have envisioned the many hundreds of other missionaries who walk the dusty streets and roads of these everlasting hills bringing the Gospel to these people". We may not need the faith to walk on water, but we do need faith to walk through tribulation and through the mud, the rain and the snow and to work so that others can progress.

"Elder and Sister Dunn were called to Peru with no prior knowledge of the spanish language. They occasionally wondered why the Lord would call them to South America where they were seemingly so ineffective and unable to use their talents. For example, they had met a young man on the street and invited him into the chapel to hear the missionary discussions. He accepted the invitation. Their spanish was such that they could only read the discussions from the manual. When the young man asked a question that they didn't understand they would just smile and keep on reading. He was later baptized and now is preparing to go on a mission.

"When the District President found out about their baptism, he asked, "How can they be baptizing, they don't even speak spanish?" But this couple did a great job and the people loved them so much. They were a strength to the members just to be there.

In the following letter dated November 12, 1986, special permission was requested from the First Presidency and later granted by President Howard W. Hunter of the Quorum of the Twelve Apostles for Elder Dunn to serve as our mission patriarch.

Elder Dunn previously served as a Patriarch in his home stake of El Centro California. His Spanish is progressing and I think that with some practice he will be able to give blessings without much difficulty. The Elders in our office staff can help him by giving backup support in transcribing the blessings as he gives them. He would be able to do the final editing.

You might be interested to know that here in the Peru Lima South Mission we have nine member districts with over fifty branches. There are over 9,500 members, many of who are desiring to receive their patriarchal blessings. However, due to economic restraints, it is difficult or they are unable to travel to Lima or a stake nearby to receive their blessings. The missionaries and members that are able to come to Lima and receive a copy of their blessings as there are many members in the local stakes who are also receiving their patriarchal blessings.

Elder Dunn had served as patriarch prior to their mission for 3 years and had given over 100 blessings. There were more than 11,000 members in our mission who, because of their distance from the stakes or the size of their district, would not be seeing a patriarch for many many years. Elder and Sister Dunn began to travel all over the mission giving Patriarchal Blessings. In the last 5 months of his mission he gave 695 beautiful Patriarchal Blessings. The first one was in English, but the rest were in Spanish!

"What a great blessing to Peru! He signed the last three blessings just before they got on the airplane to return home from their mission. This was an historical event in Peru and part of a great blessing that they, along with the many other noble and wonderful missionary couples, had given Peru through their service.

"Elder Jose Bravo, who had served as the Branch President for 6 months and was one of two Peruvian missionary couples soon to receive another assignment elsewhere in the mission. He was concerned that no one was ready or worthy to be branch president. I promised him that the Lord would indicate his choice if we did our part. After interviewing and praying to the Lord for guidance, my secretary, Brother Julio Trujillo, a returned missionary and secretary to the mission presidency, and I were both impressed that Brother Navarro was the man the Lord had chosen. He had been a member for only two months and at that moment was being ordained a priest in the next room.

"We again interviewed him and reminded him that in answer to our questions in our first interview he had told us that he was willing to do anything for the Lord. He had no idea what was in store for him. He once again bore his testimony and commitment to the church. I then said, "Brother Navarro, the Lord has called you to be the Branch President of the Nazca Branch."

"His eyes got large and he said, "¿Como jefe de los Mormones en Nazca?" "Yes", I said, "as the leader of the Mormons in Nazca." He then looked above us into the air as he contemplated my words. It was several minutes before anyone spoke. We watched him have a spiritual experience as his mind was opened up to what this calling meant. Then he looked into my eyes and said with resolve, "President Christensen, I will accept the call. I don't know what I need to do or how to do it, but I know the Lord will help me." I explained that his first assignment was to fast and pray to choose his counselors. The following week Brother Trujillo would return to set them apart and answer his questions about the handbook he was to read during the week.

"That day, he was wearing a casual sports shirt which was unbuttoned at the collar. The next Sunday he came with his counselors in white shirts and ties. He served for many years as one of the outstanding branch presidents in the mission.

It was not uncommon to have members, missionaries and new converts relate the special spiritual experiences relating to their conversion, ministry or requests for divine intervention. "During July 1984, in a letter to President Christensen, Elder Lucas shared a special experience that took place in Nayca. He wrote as follows: "President: My experience with the angels is like this. I got up around 4:00 a.m. to go to the bathroom. Upon opening my eyes I saw a personage dressed in white. I wanted to see him good, but I couldn't anymore and in the morning, I told that to my companion. He told me before I saw the personage he had thrown out Satan, because he wanted to overpower my companion. He raised his hand in the form to baptize and said, "In the name of Jesus Christ I command you to leave." Now we understand that the Lord took care of us with His angels. I am happy to be a missionary and for the blessings that God gives me. I testify of this in the name of Jesus Christ. Amen."

All four elders went on to San Ramon and then they split up. Elder Tim Shields and Elder Pedro Benites went into Oxapampa to work with Elder Morales and Elder Malca. They were not able to go to Pozuzo because of the huaycos (mud slides). Once, the jeep stalled in the middle of a river. Luckily, Elder Benites was a mechanic and dried the wires and distributor cap to allow them to move on. They were trapped for four days behind a huayco and finally got out to return to San Ramon and then to Tarma and to Lima. They spent quite a bit of time in their truck, in the jeep, and were happy to get home.

Elder Petersen and Elder Jones went into Satipo with two cases of copies of the Book of Mormon and a case of pamphlets. They had a wonderful time in that they sold all their copies of the Book of Mormon and placed all of their folletos within three or four hours. That night they had charlas with several families and found the city to be very receptive and ready for the Gospel. They said that there were 20 people with money in their hand who wanted to buy a copy of the Book of Mormon, but they didn't have anymore. One young man with whom they had a discussion with that night had tears in his eyes and said that the Gospel is true. He told them that he had been studying the Catholic Church and knew that it wasn't the Lord's true church. Now he and wanted to know how he could become a member of the Mormon Church.

The night before, they had gone into a cornfield and had blessed the city of Satipo for receiving the Gospel. That evening, after their day's labor, they saw a miraculous sight when they passed through the Plaza de Armas in downtown Satipo. On every bench there was a person reading the Book of Mormon or a pamphlet. They returned to Lima rejoicing for their success. They both had been very sick during this time with diarrhea, but had gone forward and worked very hard in spite of it all.

In an article written in a Chincha newspaper (1985), we were accused of being sons of the Devil, spies from the United States, racists, non-Christian, and of having money as our God. The newspaper that wrote the article made a practice of writing articles for those who paid and then receiving money from those they defamed to counter the accusations. President Hinckley had counseled church members not to contend with our enemies so President Christensen counseled the members and missionaries to do nothing but continue to preach the Gospel to everyone. In a zone conference in Tarma, President Christensen made the statement that "Everyone can change and everyone needs the Gospel. Even those who write such things will someday be converted."

Several months later, at our Monday night farewell dinner, Elder Gorge Olivera, from Cuzco, reminded the mission president of the statement he had made in Tarma and then described how one of the authors of the article that had been written in Chincha had come to the Church to try to write more bad things and to try to get us to retaliate. Elder Olivera and his companion, Elder Velarde, talked to him and gave him a copy of the Book of Mormon. At first they were a little afraid of him, but later he looked for them and asked to be baptized.

As a result of his conversion, Brother Severiano Francia Alvarez lost his job at the newspaper. This was not a small sacrifice due to the high rate of unemployment in Peru. But he couldn't convince his employers that they were doing something terribly wrong. His family and many friends had the discussions and may also have joined the Church.

On April 28, 1985, the Cuzco Stake was formed by Elder Howard W. Hunter. The May 12th issue of the "Church News" had the following article:

A stake has been created where once stood the headquarters of the mighty Inca empire that stretched across the boundaries of six present-day countries.

Machu P:ichu, one of south America's most visited ruins, is located within the boundaries of the stake, some 50 miles northwest of Cuzco.

The formation of the Cuzco Peru Stake is a significant milestone for the Church, said Elder Howard W. Hunter of the Council of the Twelve, who organized the stake of more than 2,300 members on April 28. Eldler Hunter, who has maintained an interest in the archaeological aspect of the area for many years, said, 'Many descendants of Incas walk along the streets today. They wear wide bowler hats. It just takes you back a long step in history. Many of our members are Inca descendants.'

Cuzco is built upon the ruins of a stone city that was once connected by a vast system of roads to Inca territories along the west coast of South America. "A stake has been created where once stood the headquarters of the mighty Inca empire that stretched across the boundaries of six present-day countries.

Macchu Pichu, one of South America's most visited ruins, is located within the boundaries of the stake, some 50 miles northwest of Cuzco.

The formation of the Cuzco , Peru Stake is a significant milestone for the Church, said Elder Howard W. Hunter of the Council of the Twelve, who organized the stake of more than 2,300 members on April 28. Elder Hunter, who has maintained an interest in the archaeological aspect of the area for many These interests included parts of what are now Colombia, Ecuador, Peru, Bolivia, Chile and Argentina. The empire, with a long and narrow shape like a modern-day Chile, had a well-developed trade economy.

One of the new Cuzco wards is in Sacsayhuaman, located at the site of an Inca fortress. This fortress is known for its walls of huge stones, some up to 16 feet high. The stones were hauled 35 miles and fitted together so tightly that a knife blade cannot be inserted between them.

Elder Hunter's interest in Cuzco began many years ago . . . 'It is a remarkable thing to now have a stake organized here,' he said."

On Page 11 of the "Church News" there was the article describing the contribution of the Peruvian missionaries:

South America North Area: Native missionaries lead way. In the Lima, Peru South Mission, negotiations are underway for the purchase of 30 meeting house properties to relieve crowding in the mission's 40 branches. The mission's rapid growth is evident in such areas as Chosica, where one struggling branch a year ago is today a ward and two healthy branches. The growth spurt can be partly attributed to more full-time local missionaries, who now number about 75 percent of the more than 270 missionaries.

These "local" Peruvian missionaries were and are among the most faithful and valiant of the world. Elders Jorge Olivera, incidently from Cuzco, and Cesar Velande are just two examples of the caliber of missionaries serving the Lord. Due to the political unrest and terrorism they were transferred sometime later. They wrote of the following of their experience opening up a new area in the altiplano:

"It was a great opportunity and challenge to be able to open the marvelous program at Huancavelica. We spent Christmas getting the necessary luggage ready for a few days to see the program, because missionaries had never gone there to open it. We got to Huancavelica at 5:30 p.m. We retrieved our luggage, and we went to look for a place to spend the night. We walked down the street and we entered a hotel. There weren't any vacancies. And likewise in the second and third hotels. Finally we found a hotel. We paid and entered, but as soon as we walked in the door of the room I said to my companion, "Let's get out of here!" My companion agreed with me, and we made the excuse that there wasn't any showers or hot water, and they gave us back our money and we left. We arrived at another hotel and we stayed there. It was a lot better and we felt tranquil. We were there for a week looking for a room, but there wasn't one.

There were a lot of policemen that were protecting the city from the "Sendero Luminoso", more commonly known as terrorists. Three days after we left from the hotel where we paid and left it was blown up by dynamite. We went to look at it. The room where we would have stayed was totally destroyed. Then we understood that the feeling that we had was not our imagination, but that it was the spirit of the Lord that was protecting us and watching over us. At first, it didn't seem like anything serious to us, but when we thought about it again, we understood better. The protection that we all have is like a glove. When the hand goes into the glove, the glove can do what it need to do, but without the hand, it lays there motionless. The spirit is the same. When we have the spirit we do what is right, but when it goes away from us, it is better to try to obtain it.

There were a lot of explosions and one was only a block away from where we were staying. The days went by in that manner. I had never used a package tricycle instead of a taxi to move the things. We traveled to Huancayo many times, and we spent many nights traveling in the bus. Because when the sun came up, we had to cross a hanging bridge to the other side to the bus that was waiting for us on the other side of the river to take us to Huancavelica. We had to do that because the terrorists blew up the bridge that the buses went across on. Those nights were really cold, and me and my companion felt happy to experience all of this being in the service of the Lord.

One day there was a curfew, but we didn't know anything about it. My companion had a change and didn't know anything about the curfew, because one morning we walked to our room and nothing happened to us. Another time we were coming from the fallen bridge to the city. It was a half an hour walk. Maybe there were terrorists or policemen in the mountains, but nevertheless, we came laughing and joking, happy to be alive. My companion's brother, who is a policeman, said that the motto of the policemen there is "We prefer suspicious people dead before alive." And that is the way that the policemen were there. We were happy to find a member of the Church who was there because of work reasons. Through him we found the room where we lived and at the same time was our chapel for our sacrament meetings of three people.

When we finally started to work, after all of this, we had a family of 12 people. Father, mother, and the children. They wanted to get baptized, and the words they said were of great satisfaction to us because another family of 8 were progressing also. These two families were a total of 20 people. They told us that since we had come into their lives they had more work, and that they weren't lacking anything. Another family of 6 was almost impossible helping them to understand the true Gospel, We gave a Book of Mormon to them, which bore testimony of itself, until they asked for their baptisms. The week that I left we were going to have 17 baptisms. My testimony has grown a lot.

December 1, 1985, "Church News" another article was published which reads as follows:

> While the turmoil of South America is often trumped in newspaper headlines, the quiet progress, especially in people's lives, goes unnoticed. In the half centurn of LDS presence on the continent, gospel progress has come to multitudes in the South America North Area countries of Bolivia, Brazil, Colombia, Ecuador, Venezuela and peru. Church membership has reached 343,000 in about 100 stakes and is now growing at a 10 percent annual rate. Last year almost a third of the Church's converts came from these countries...
>
> On the continent's west coast, the Cuzco, Peru Stake has been created at the headquarters of the once-powerful Inca Empire, near the famed ruins of Macchu Pichu. Stakes for Inca descendants have been created among Quichua-speaking Otavalo Indians in the dense rain forests of Ecuador, and among Aymara and Quechua-speaking residents of Bolivia's 13,000 foot high altiplano area. Bolivia La Paz Stake members note that theirs is the highest stake in the world, and add, "We're the closest to heaven.
>
> South America's third temple will soon be dedicated in Lima, Peru. Two stakes have been established at Iquitos, Peru at the head waters of the Amazon River...
>
> In outlining the challenges facing South American members, Elders I. Burton Howard and Helio Camargo said the toughest challenge is economics. Sparse economic resources mean few telephones. In some stakes, the combined membership owns no more than half a dozen cars. Because public transportation is reduced on Sundays, members occasionally wait hours for bus connections. A trip across town to a meeting house can be an all-day project...

The (Area) Presidency hopes to maintain the growth rate in the future, but foster it at centers of strength were resources can be concentrated

On December 1, 1985, the Area Presidency wrote this memorandum describing how we should be establishing, maintaining and growing from centers of strength:

For Church purposes this term (centers of strength) is used today to mean a stake, no more and no less. The Lord said he would establish his Church and build it up. (D&C 10:53-54) Stakes are appointed or established for the righteous to gather in. (D&C 109:39,59) Stakes serve as a refuge from the storm. (D&C 115:6) Stakes are the "strength of the Church". (D&C 101:21) They must be strengthened (D&C 82:14), that Zion may go forth. (D&C 133:9)

The fact that the Lord has counseled us to strengthen the stakes means that the stakes are not as strong as they could be. A stake is no stronger than its wards. If wards lack leadership, do not offer the full program of the Church, or are scattered and small, then stakes will be the same. On the other hand, if wards are well staffed, have trained and experienced leaders, then all of the Gospel, provide activities and opportunities for growth and development to their members, then stakes will be strong. Experience has demonstrated that these things happen primarily in centers of strength, or in other words, in stakes...

To insure that strong stakes are established in accordance with these guidelines beginning January 1, 1986, the Area Presidency suggests that the names and callings of key priesthood leaders be included with all new unit applications, together with the names of others who are prepared and who might be able to serve in similar positions if called should these units be divided. "This Priesthood Organization Report", together with a copy of the latest Quarterly Statistical Report of the stake and the appropriate ward or stake division application with attachments, should be endorsed by the Mission President and submitted to the Area Presidency by the Regional Representative before division will be approved.

Careful attention should be given to planning future stakes on the basis of the relative closeness of the units so the wards can act like wards and the units are close enough together so the stakes can act like stakes. This will mean taking into account centers of member and non-member population as well as joint plans by the Mission President, Stake President and Regional Representative as to where to concentrate the full-time and stake missionary work. Isolated wards and branches might have to get along as best they can for the time being as we concentrate our missionary effort in those places where the members and non-members are in sufficient numbers to establish centers of Church strength and where wards or potential wards are close enough together to offer members of the Church the full Church program. In some cases these centers will not offer as rapid growth as some other areas, but they will offer Church strength and leadership necessary to take care of some of the less developed units. This is what is meant by growing from positions of strength and we need to grow in this manner...

In order to maintain strong wards and stakes, it is essential that leaders be properly trained and remain in office for a sufficient time to build and establish the fundamental programs of the Church. These include: 1) Multiple occupancy of building. 2) Tenure - Church leaders are not called for specific terms, however, mature stakes in Latin America should encourage their leaders to stay in office as long as possible and not release themselves from positions to which they were called by the Lord.

Priesthood leaders in centers of strength must administer the Gospel. (D&C 84:19) This means that: 1) Priesthood leadership positions must be filled. 2) Priesthood Executive Committee meetings must be held weekly. 3) Leaders must establish a sound financial base. 4) A permanent ward mission leader should be called and trained by and under the direction of the Stake Presidency. 5) Home teaching and visiting teaching should be established. 6) Honest and timely reports should be filed at all levels. Leaders should be prepared to report their stewardship in these areas regularly.

Mission President's Resource No. 12 sets forth several useful principles in assigning missionaries effectively and efficiently to work in centers of strength. There the following points are emphasized: 1) Assign missionaries to areas of high member density; 2) Concentrate on finding activities; 3) Where feasible assign missionaries in more populated areas where literary and economic status are higher. As a strong, viable nucleus of leadership is established missionary work can then be expanded in every widening circles; and 4) New areas are to be opened only after receiving written approval from the Area Presidency.

When the principles set forth above are not followed, division often results in two weak stakes instead of one (strong stake). There is danger that the branches will overpower the roots. (Jacob 5:48)

In the June of 1986, President Milton Alvin Romney and Sister Lucile Turley Romney arrived in Lima to open up the new Missionary Training Center (MTC). They received their first missionaries on July 3rd and give instructions for a twelve day period to a new group of missionaries arriving twice a month. This new training center was to prepare missionaries from Peru, Bolivia, Ecuador and Colombia. The Peru Lima South mission home was converted into the training center and housing fore these missionaries. Brother Jay Jensen came from the Missionary Department in Salt Lake City to assist with the first group of missionaries. The Romneys were replace in January 1988 by President Leon and Sister Zeona Walker and they were followed by President Bruce and Sister Rowene Gibson.

In a letter from the Area Presidency dated August 1, 1986, church leaders in Peru were instructed to take certain measures to become self sufficient. The described steps outline the procedure to comply with the fourth requirement that:

To prepare the Church to take the Gospel to parts of the world that has never had the missionaries, it's necessary to consider that which the Church in South America, and especially in the Andean area, can do to help in this very important undertaking.

We are conforming with the counsel of the prophets and under the direction of the Quorum of the Twelve, who have asked us to augment our self sufficiency to a level never before seen. This means that the Church in South America ought to depend less on the financial and personal help and other material resources from the general offices of the Church, and at the same time, too conserve and even expand the saving programs of preaching the Gospel, perfecting the saints, and redeeming the dead.

The following procedures will help: 1) As soon as possible, we ought to do what is necessary to reduce the cost of the buildings and maintenance of those buildings. 2) We need to begin now to raise the total level of complying with the payment of titling. 3) Beginning the First of January 1987, the young men and women need to contribute at least one third of the cost of their mission, and more if possible, as a condition to receive a calling to serve as full-time missionaries. 4) The stakes can no longer use fast offerings other than those generated among members of the same stake. In Doctrine & Covenants, the Lord has said that the Church ought to "stand independent above all other creatures beneath the celestial world." (D&C 78:14)

However, in becoming independent, the services of experienced latter-day saints was of great value in teaching these principles to new members. In a letter dated September 8, 1986, written by President Dale Christensen to all the Missionary Couples at the MTC shares the following conversion of the Torres family as told by Elder and Sister Lyon. It read as follows:

Elder and Sister Lyon arrived in the Peru Lima South Mission and in the first proselytizing area in Chosica, they taught the charlas to the Torres family. Ten days later they baptized the whole family. In a letter to me they said, "Elder Huayta and Olivera accompanied us to the house as it is on a high-ridged street. The rooms were all full of beds so we sat on a bed. I gave the charla, and afterwards, the mother and one of the daughters said a dark-complexioned man had been standing in the room all the time I was talking.

We continued giving them a charla daily to the family without seeing the father. On the fifth charla I encountered the father, and he gave written permission for all the family to be baptized. We gave the first three charlas to the father and you could feel the presence of the Holy Ghost. The father began to cry, the family felt it also at this time.

The father was taught the rest of the charlas and the family was baptized as a whole. The father and the family were baptized the following day, Sunday, July 27; the tenth day of our mission and the tenth day of our beginning the charlas. It was a very special experience for all involved, and we were happy to have played a small role in the conversion. We had to teach by the spirit as our Spanish was not too good. I read the charlas and the Holy Ghost taught."

The Lyon's had another baptism. A twenty-eight year old man who listened to the discussions. They also baptized the wife of a long-standing member who finally accepted the invitation to see the film "Christ in America" and listen to the charlas. The Lyon's stated in the same letter, "During the first charla she would not read the Scriptures or pray. Her husband did it all at her insistence. The second charla went much better. She read the Scriptures while her husband held the baby. The spirit was so strong that as we turned to go, Darlene tried to say, 'You have a beautiful family'. The woman began to cry and said, 'Why is it that every time you are here, I feel such a strong spirit?' We testified to her that it was the Holy Ghost testifying to her of the truthfulness of our message. She did not seem to want us to go, so we stayed and visited. She asked us to come back and finish the charlas . . . so poco a poco progress is being made."

In October, President Christensen requested ten couples with a good knowledge of the Spanish language and familiarity with the General Handbook of Instructions, gospel principles, and other handbooks and manuals as well. If possible, also with knowledge of welfare principles. Included was a quote from the following letter dated October 15, 1985 from Elder Scott T. Lyman and Sister Lyn M. Lyman (a missionary couple serving in the Peru Lima South Mission) to help in the request:

We would plead for more couples to serve as missionaries. A couple assigned to a new district or stake, or even to a struggling branch for three or four months, would lend expertise and spiritual reinforcement of inestimable value to the inexperience leaders of these units. There are High Priest quorums of over fifty members in some wards in Utah, with wives equally qualified, constituting a great untapped reservoir of experience and testimony. We feel such a quorum would hardly miss ten or fifteen couples serving in the frontiers of the Church, and the mission work would progress tremendously. We recommend a concerted effort to recruit mature couples from all parts of the world to renew their youth through missionary service.

On November 12, 1986, President Christensen wrote the following letter to the First Presidency requesting approval for Elder Marcel Dunn to serve as Patriarch for the Peru Lima South Mission:

. . . Elder Dunn previously served as a Patriarch in his home stake of El Centro California. His Spanish is progressing, and I think that with some practice he will be able to give blessings without much difficulty. The Elders in our office staff can help him by giving backup support in transcribing the blessings as he gives them. He would be able to do the final editing.

You might be interested to know that here in the Peru Lima South Mission we have nine member districts with over fifty branches. There are over 9,500 members, many of which are desiring to receive their patriarchal blessings. The missionaries and members that are able to come to Lima and receive their blessings have waited for six months to a year to receive a copy of their blessing as there are many members in the local stakes who are also receiving their patriarchal blessings . . .

The Area Presidency supported this request and on December 16, 1986 we the following response from President Howard W. Hunter, President of the Quorum of Twelve Apostles:

This letter will authorize Elder Marcel Dunn, an ordained patriarch, to give patriarchal blessings to worthy members in districts and branches in the mission while serving as a proselyting missionary with his wife.

In authorizing Elder Dunn to give these blessings to worthy members, branch and district leaders should be advised that he is not to give blessings to members who are too new to understand the significance of a patriarchal blessing. They shoud be in the Church at least one year.

We trust that this will be a great blessing to the Saints of the Peru Lima South Mission.

The special experience of hiking the Inca Trail for three days and two nights (June 9-11, 1986) was an appreciation preparation experience for President and Sister Christensen. They were able to coordinate with Elder Loren C. Dunn's schedule around stake and zone conferences and Alex's, his son, school schedule. While enjoying the experience they continued to share the gospel. In a letter dated November 25, 1986, to President Loren C. Dunn I related the following event:

This last week, during interviews with the missionaries, I was told by the Elders, of the conversion of a particular family. Evidently, we met some of the children in a narrow street one night as we walked, with you and Sister Dunn, from the restaurant to the hotel. We talked briefly and I gave them our card. The next day the missionaries taught the family another discussion and the child told them they "met a missionary with his father." The missionaries couldn't imagine who it was until they saw the card. They reported a strong, wonderful conversion, and baptism of the whole entire family. Just thought you would all like to know that.

Chapter 13

DEDICATION: Lima Peru Temple

While the temple was under construction, the Saints were being prepared to be able to attend it after its dedication. They were taught to put their lives in order and to qualify themselves for a temple recommend. They also would need to prepare their family records in order to perform the ordinances for themselves, their families and their deceased ancestors. Missionary couples were called to assist with this preparation. Elder and Sister Albert Means helped to organize stake genealogical leaders (usually husband and wife) in each of the 12 stakes in Lima. In August of 1984, Elder Malcolm and Sister Mary Wilding were authorized by Elder Robert E. Wells of the Presidency of the South America North Area to function in this program throughout all of Peru. They were also in charge of the Extraction Program in Lima.

A special sacrament meeting programs were prepared for all the stakes and missions during the month of October (28th). A special fast in November (4th) was intended to obtain help in obtaining family records. Workshops were set up and held in over forty cities to assist members to complete their first and second generation family group sheets.

Many faith promoting experiences took place during the preparation of the genealogical records. Through dreams, visions, and the great faith of the wonderful Peruvian saints, much needed information was made available.

One example of sacrifice and dedication to attend these workshops was given by Brother Marcos Barbaran and his friend, a former missionary to Peru from Minnesota, USA. They worked in a gold-mining operation in the jungle along the Amazon River. To attend the workshop, they needed to come to boat into Puerto Maldonado. It would take three days and they could not spare that much time from work. Instead, they made the trip in one day by walking through dense jungle paths and wading in alligator infested swamps. After getting the dates and other information from his family in Iquitos by Telex, he was able to complete his own family group sheet.

Another sister in Tacna remembered as a child seeing her uncle write in a notebook the genealogy and history of the family. As she grew older and after becoming a member of the church, she realized the importance of the book and wanted to borrow it. However, he refused her request because she was a Mormon. She fasted and every night she prayed that he would let her have it. One night as she prayed and cried, a sweet peaceful feeling came and a voice inside told her not to worry that she would be able to get it. Within a few days the mailman came to her door with a brown envelope and inside was the notebook. She was so thrilled and her mother began to copy it into another book. Her uncle sent work to her that she could have it because none of his children were interested in it and she had always had such an interest in the family history.

At the workshop, she also related a dream where she was in a room with lots of papers, books and records. Two women were there who wanted her to do something for them. There were very distinct in characteristics and appearance. When she told the dream to her mother and described these women, she was told that they were her two dead aunts. She had never seen them in person or in a picture. Her patriarchal blessing promised her that her ancestors had accepted the Gospel in the spirit world and were waiting for her to do their work.

At another workshop one brother did not have the birthdate of his father. The next day he had it. He related to the group that the night before he had a dream where a man took him to a book and said, "Look and read this." There was the date he needed.

Brother Handa, of the Central Ward of the Lima Central Stake, did not know what part of Japan his grandparents had come from. He prayed and contacted the Japanese Embassy in Lima and was given the name of a city where people had his last name. He wrote to the city and received a response. One day a knock came to the door and there stood a young man in his early twenties. He was brother Handa's nephew from Japan. He came with all the genealogical data. Until that moment, he had been a complete stranger whom Brother Handa had never seen nor known about. The genealogy was written in Japanese. Brother Handa could not read it and his nephew could not speak Spanish. With the help of a friend it was translated.

Brother Santos Donato Bautisa Chico showed found that his father, mother and five brothers and sisters had been killed in the May 31, 1970 earthquake in Yungay. He was only twelve years old then, the youngest member and only survivor of his family. After his baptism, he was thrilled to be helped by others to complete the family group sheets.

A special satisfaction and gratitude came from all those who could not read or write. Through this extraction program, special fasts and workshops many received their sacred temple ordinances. At this time, Sister Nubia Stromsdorfer eas serving as the Director of the Extraction Program, Brother Prospero Villanueva as Director of the Genealogical Service Center and Eduardo Cordara presided over the Genealogical Organization of the stakes in Lima.

In preparation of the dedication of the Lima Peru Temple the following letters, dated December 9, 1985, were sent to all local priesthood leaders who read it in Sacrament meeting, and carried it to the homes of members. They read as follows:

As the time for the dedication of the Lima Peru Temple approaches, we call upon all members of the Church within the Lima Peru Temple District to prepare their hearts and minds for this historic event. In doing so, we urge them to use this occasion as an opportunity to cleanse their lives of anything that is displeasing to the Lord, eliminating from their hearts, any ill feelings and feelings of envy or enmity and seeking forgiveness for anything that is amiss in their lives.

As an aid in seeking this objective, we urge that the Fast Day in January be used to focus upon the great blessings that emanate from temples and temple work. Also, we urge families to focus upon the same theme during family home evenings to be held the first week in January. Individual members should do the same in their secret prayers, imploring the Lord for increased spirituality and dedication, especially dedication to temple work and genealogical research.

The dedication of the Lima Peru Temple has been announced and is scheduled to be held on Friday, Saturday, and Sunday, January 10, 11 and 12, 1986. The public viewing during the open house period will begin December 10, 1985, and will last until December 21, 1985. A cornerstone service will be held at 9:30 a.m. on Friday, January 10, 1986, and the first dedicatory session will commence immediately following the Cornerstone Ceremony. The Dedicatory service will be repeated in ten successive sessions as listed. . .

It was explained by President Hinckley that there are various ceremonies related to the dedication of the temple. First of all there is a ground breaking ceremony. Secondly there would be a sealing of the history of artifacts in a cornerstone. Then the actual dedicatory prayer.

Elder James E. Faust: We come humbly with our hearts full of joy. We have very many different cultures and races as described in Ephesians 4:19-20. If the temple is to achieve the glory that is intended there needs to be a cornerstone. Perhaps the day will come when the Savior will come to Lima and He himself will enter this House.

When that day comes where the living and dead, because we do work for the both of them in this temple, let the trumpets sound and let us be caught up in a cloud to meet Him. May this holy work continue in glory and in power and in beauty from everlasting to everlasting in the name of Jesus Christ, Amen.

Elder F. Burton Howard: There is a saying in Spanish, "A ver es una cosa, ver alli es otro." (To see is one thing, to see them is another.) In Second Nephi he quoted where the temples are the foundations of salvation.

President Gordon B. Hinckley: What a beautiful building with all the beautiful furniture. Since I have arrived her I have not been able to hold back the tears. We arrived this morning at 3:30 a.m. Our plane was quite late, but as we have come we have seen the beauty of this temple and have been caught with the emotion of it. We have here a copper box with documents about Peru. Perhaps in 100 years it will be opened to know about what happened now. (President Hinckley told of the account when he traveled by train from Cuzco to Puno and then to Juliaca to cross the Lake Titicaca in a boat built in 1904 in Leads, England. It was floated then across the Atlantic through the Panama Canal and through the Pacific and then transported by train to Lake Titicaca. He told of his feelings for the Lamanite People as he traveled across Lake Titicaca to La Paz in Bolivia and his love for the people and how he felt Father Lehi was crying to the Lord asking him how long it would be before the people would receive the blessings promised in the Book of Mormon.

Then President Gordon B. Hinckley offered the dedicatory prayer. The choir sang the Hallelujah Chorus, and waved the white handkerchief for the Hallelujah and then all sang "The Spirit of God Like A Fire is Burning."

Elder Faust: We should never be the same after participating in these sacred services. We should be as those who have walked from the darkness into the light. Many people have offered tithes and offerings to sacrifice for this sacred temple. The Priesthood is a restraining influence. Husbands with the Priesthood have no right to abuse their wives or families. It's alright to be firm, if we show much more love afterwards." (Then he told about Nebuchadnezzar's dream and how Shadrach, Meshach and Abednego were thrown into the fiery furnace that when the king looked into the furnace he saw not three young men but four. That fourth was the Spirit of the Lord. He told us how in our homes there should always be one other person, how we should always have the Spirit of the Lord with us.)

Elder Loren C. Dunn: Elder Dunn taught us of our heritage and how in the Salt Lake Temple, his grandfather, his father and he had all been sealed. And now his son is of age to be sealed in the Salt Lake Temple. He indicated that sermons are not as strong as good examples. The fathers taught by example, not by preaching. The children when taught like this will learn to love the things that the parents do. He read then from Deuteronomy chapter 4 how Moses talked to Ancient Israel and to our sons and our sons' sons and our great grand sons. They will come to love what we do and what we respect. They will do much more from our example than by our words. See also chapter 6.

President Gordon B. Hinckley: He told of his early reading, in his youth, that of the conquest of Peru. How he remembered reading of this history of pain and treachery and bondage of the inhabitants of this continent. How from the results of that book he developed a great compassion and love that has never left his heart. And he promised how this is a great day of glory, this is a day of fulfillment and prophecy, "We have passed from death into life because we have loved our brethren."

We were inspired and taught by a prophet of the Lord and encouraged to teach our investigators so they would not fall away as did Ammon in the Book of Mormon. He also challenged all the Peruvians to learn English so they could hear the words of the Prophet in his own tongue.

The January 19, 1986 issue of the <u>Church News</u> highlighted the dedication of the Lima Peru Temple:

<u>Temple prayer promises of the priesthood:</u> Following is the dedicatory prayer given by President Gordon B. Hinckley, first counselor in the First Presidency, in the dedication of the Lima Peru Temple on January 10, 1986:

God of our fathers, thou great Elohim, we come unto thee in the name of thy Beloved Son Jesus Christ, the Savior and Redeemer of the world.

We look to thee as we dedicate thy holy house. Our hearts are filled with gratitude. We love thee, and we love thy Son. Wilt thou hear our prayer, dear Father.

We thank thee for this glorious day in the history of thy work. We thank thee for this temple in the nation of Peru. We thank thee for all who have contributed to make it possible. We thank thee for thy smiles of favor upon the people of this land, and particularly upon the many who have accepted the restored Gospel as it has been taught to them. Reward their faith. Let them feel of thy love for them. Increase their knowledge of things divine. Prosper them in their labors.

Surely father Lehi has wept with sorrow over his posterity. Surely he weeps today with gladness, for in his holy house there will be experienced the fullness of the priesthood to the blessing, not only of those of this and future generations, but also to the blessing of those of previous generations.

Let thy people rejoice at the wondrous gift thou hast bestowed upon them. May they be faithful unto thee that they may be found worthy always to enter this thy house and partake of the blessings here to be offered. Through the ordinances to be performed in this house, under authority of the everlasting priesthood, they now have available every gift for time and eternity that thou hast bestowed in this the dispensation of the fullness of times.

O God, we thank thee for this glad season when thy house is complete and when we dedicate it unto thee and unto thy Beloved Son. Acting in the authority of the Holy Priesthood, which thou hast given us, thy sons, we dedicate unto thee and unto Him this the Lima Peru Temple of the Church of Jesus Christ of Latter-day Saints. We dedicate the grounds of the building. We dedicate the ancillary structure, the fittings, the furnishings, and all of the facilities connected with this sacred edifice. We dedicate this temple as thy holy sanctuary, and pray that thou wilt accept it as our offering unto thee. Wilt thou be pleased to honor it with thy presence, and to bless it and all who use it.

O God, preserve this thy holy house. Save it from the storms of nature, from the tremblings of the earth, and from the defilement of men. It is consecrated in holiness to thee, and so may it stand through generations yet to come.

May it be the means of accomplishing thine eternal purposes. May it be a house of prayer, a house of learning, a house of faith, a house of God. May all who enter its doors do so with clean hands and with hearts free from iniquity. May their numbers increase through the years and may a glorious work be here performed for the eternal blessing of the generations of men and women who have walked the earth.

Restrain the adversary that he shall not have power over thy people or over thy work. Thwart the designs of any who would do injury to the kingdom. Bless this nation and its neighbor nations which have befriended they servants. Bless those who govern that they may do so with equity, extending to the people that freedom which is consistent with thy divine plan.

Prosper thy faithful saints as they live honestly with thee in the payment of their tithes and offerings. May they enjoy the bounties of the earth as well as the blessings of heaven. Let thy Holy Spirit go before those who serve as missionaries. Open the doors and the hearts of the people. May they be responsive to the truth. Bless thy work that it shall blossom and grow in this nation and in its neighbor nations of South America. Remember, Father, thine ancient covenant with the children of Lehi that in the latter days thou wouldst favor them and bring to them a knowledge of their Redeemer. Make them strong in faith and magnify them in leadership in thy kingdom.

Prosper thy work in all the earth that it may move forward with great power to the blessing of all who shall hear the message of salvation. Smile on thy prophet, Ezra Taft Benson, and grant him health and revelation. Bless all who labor with him in promoting thy work and building thy kingdom. Bless all who have taken upon themselves the name of thy Beloved Son. May they walk as thy favored children, exemplifying in their lives the beauties of thine everlasting truth.

We thank thee, we love thee, we praise thy Holy Name. On this day of dedication, we rededicate ourselves, our lives, and all that we have and are to thee our God, with our prayer that we may be found worthy in thy sight to receive thy blessings and thy divine approbation. All of this we do in the name of thy Beloved Son, the Savior of the world, even our Redeemer, Jesus Christ, Amen.

John L. Hart wrote the following articles in the Church News (Lima, Peru):

1) Nearly 10,000 members from the highlands of Peru and Bolivia heard President Gordon B. Hinckley call the dedication of the Lima Peru Temple a fulfillment of prophecy and the answer to the prayers of the many children of Lehi.

The temple was dedicated in 11 sessions January 10-12, during the clear days of summer in the southern hemisphere.

Participating with President Hinckley were Elder James E. Faust of the Council of the Twelve and Elder Robert L. Simpson of the First Quorum of Seventy, and the South American North Area presidency, Elders F. Burton Howard, Loren C. Dunn, and Helio Camargo, who are also members of the First Quorum of Seventy.

President Hinckley frequently mentioned how he and other Church leaders had visited this area several decades earlier, and how they fervently prayed the gospel might come to lighten the load and light the lives of descendants of Father Lehi.

President Hinckley said this dedication emphasized the great progress that is being made among the people of this area.

Many members traveled up to 15 hours in buses to the temple site, which is on the outskirts of Lima. They came from the rain forests on the east side of the Andes and from the southern deserts, an area once encompassed by the Inca Empire . . .

The Buenos Aires temple was dedicated in 11 sessions on January 17-19 . . .

2) Sergio Gomez was helping to build the kingdom while helping to build the temple in Lima. Gomez, a Brazilian and project representative for the Church Physical Facilities Department, has been spreading the gospel while

supervising the temple's construction, said President Dale Christensen of the Peru Lima South Mission.

As far as he is aware, Gomez was responsible this past year for more pamphlets and copies of the Book of Mormon being placed, more discussions being taught, and more conversions than any person in the mission.

Gomez often invited missionaries to show filmstrips to construction workers during the laborers' lunch hours, or sent missionaries to the workers' homes in the evenings.

At least 50 people joined the Church as a result of Gomez' efforts.

3) Genealogists here could easily date their work as being completed either B.T. or A.T. -- before temple or after temple.

Before the temple, genealogy work was mostly stored away in a closet, like the microfilm readers at the office of Prospero Villanueva Rodriguez, supervisor of genealogical services in Peru. His office was tucked upstairs in a tiny room of the distribution center. Only a few devoted genealogists researched their heritage there.

After the temple, interest in genealogy work couldn't be more different, according to Church leaders. A majority of active members seem to be driven, with four-generation sheets in hand, to seek their forefathers. . .

4) Members are looking deeper into their own lives as they prepare for a temple recommend interview. One active member grew tearful and declined a recommend. The mission president learned that she felt unworthy only because she wasn't having family home evening regularly.

Also, a few of the rather well-to-do people living in the community surrounding the temple were joining the Church. It's very hard to arrange missionary meetings because you have to ring at the gate and speak to a maid. In the past we've had little success in the area. In the last six months, however, that area has been as busy and successful as any other area in the mission. . .

In the January 26, 1986 issue of the Church News on pages 3 and 7, was the article by John L. Hart titled "Temples received with thanks. Prophecy fulfilled for Peru members":

> Not since the Inca Empire was conquered four and a half centuries ago has a temple been erected in the northern regions of the Andes. This temple, however, has been built and dedicated "to the glory of God," fulfilling prophecy and answering prayers, said Church leaders.
>
> This is the day for which people on both sides of the veil have prayed," said President Gordon B. Hinckley, first counselor in the First Presidency, who dedicated the temple. "No wonder we sing hallelujah . . . God is remembering His covenant people in the highlands of the Andes. . ."
>
> The dedication was an unpublicized event, perhaps unnoticed in the city except by drivers who found their buses to and from the temple clogged with well-dressed members.
>
> Some members came by airplane 350 miles from the northeast -- the only way of travel out of the steamy Amazon rain forests that surround Iquitos, Peru. Others rode buses from as far as Tacna, about 400 miles away in the desert south, and by truck and car from other areas. A busload of Bolivians traveled two days and overcame washed-out bridges near the Bolivian border to attend services on Sunday, January 12.
>
> In attendance were professionals in medicine, law and business, as well as others with less-formal education. All described the dedication as a "beautiful experience." Francisco Vega Machacuay came with his wife and baby from the rugged, mountainous Cerro de Pasco mining district about 100 miles east of Lima. The family made the 10-hour trip in the back of a truck. "This is the temple of the Lord," he said. "We have 25 members in our Carhuamayo Branch. I think the new temple will help them." He concluded saying, "Salutations to all in the

Church for us in the name of the Lord. We send our love. . ."

The members' presence was inspiring to leaders. After two days of dedicatory sessions, President Hinckley remarked, "As I look into your faces today . . . I see men of power and capacity; I see women of strength and beauty. I know the Lord is moving among this people to redeem them and to bring light and industry in their lives, wisdom in their minds, to rear leaders among them -- men who hold and honor the priesthood."

He said that as he looked at the temple, "I was so pleased I couldn't hold back the tears and I haven't been able to hold them back since. There stands now a House of the Lord in the nation of Peru. God be thanked for this glorious and happy day."

Elder James E. Faust of the Council of the Twelve said the temple will be a blessing to Peru. "Every temple diminishes the power of Satan and increases the power of God."

He said the Lord has blessed the descendants of Lehi. "We were here when there was nothing. Now there are stakes in all these lands." It is as though, he said, the people are pre-programmed, like computers, toward the gospel. "The Lord's name is already written on your inward parts. . ."

Also speaking were Elders Robert L. Simpson, F. Burton Howard, Loren C. Dunn and Helio Camargo of the First Quorum of Seventy. . .

Another article titled "Hopes of generations realized at South American dedications" by John L. Hart read as follows:

. . .Members accustomed to sacrifice are asked to sacrifice yet more. Not from their tables, or from their family welfare: something else, something special.

In Peru, where many workers earn less than $8 a day, personal possessions were donated, Church leaders said.

Members sold television sets and stereos. Some auctioned furniture. Some of the men had gold fillings pried from their teeth and replaced with a less costly substance. Wives slipped gold wedding bands from their fingers and handed them to their bishop . . . Mario Perotti, temple committee chairman in Peru, put members' feelings into perspective: "The conquistadores searched in the jungle for gold, but they found none. We now have a greater place to search. Here is our gold, here in the temple."

The March 1986 issue of the Ensign carried the following article:

> In remarks before the dedicatory prayer, President Hinckley spoke of "another congregation" looking down on the proceedings. "I always feel during a dedication that I am standing in two spheres with a very thin veil."
>
> He told of past trips in Peru and Bolivia when he had seen the children of Lehi in poverty, oppressed in spirit by the scarcity of gospel truth among them, and cried within himself, "How long, oh Lord, how long?"
>
> "The day has arrived. Lehi, Sariah, Nephi and others in that other sphere are rejoicing. This is the day of salvation for generations," President Hinckley said. . .
>
> "When I heard the opening prayer in the cornerstone ceremony, I felt the presence of the Lord. It was the same spirit I felt when I left on my mission and when my husband and I were sealed in the temple," commented Beatrice Casos de Millan, Primary president in the Lima Peru Magdalena Stake.
>
> During the dedicatory service, "we all felt close to the Lord," said Pedro Chinchay, financial clerk for the Lima Peru Limatambo Stake. "As it says in the scriptures, the

Lamanites will blossom as a rose. (See D&C 49:24) For me, the temple is an indication that that day is coming."

Members were not the only ones on whom the temple made a deep impression. The open house was extended by three days because of public interest; more than 24,500 people streamed through the temple between December 11 and December 28.

One, a representative of the president of the Peruvian congress, said he had visited the temple site two weeks earlier on assignment to learn what kind of building was being constructed. He reported then that it was "a beautiful building with religious purposes." But, he added, "Today when I entered the grounds I felt the greatest sensation of peace I have ever felt in my life. My report will be that within these walls one feels the love of your members and the love of God."

The mayor of La Molina, the suburban community where the temple is located, commented: "I believe that God is pleased with this work, and I am sure he smiles with satisfaction to see such a select group of people working for the welfare of his children." His wife, touched by "the love of God" she felt in the temple and among members meeting the public there, added, "If heaven really exists, today I have visited a little piece of that heaven."

The Church News published a beautiful article about President and Sister Samuel Boren, the first Temple President and Temple Matron to preside over and serve in the Lima Peru Temple. It read as follows:

Samuel Boren, a native of Buenos Aires, Argentina, and former president of three missions, has been called as president of the Lima Peru Temple. The temple is nearing completion with the dedication expected in early 1986.

President Boren, a CPA, is retired executive director of the Housing Authority of Mesa, Arizona. His wife, Clara, a former member of the Relief Society General Board, will be temple matron.

President Boren, an ordinance worker in the Arizona Temple, has presided over the Mexico Veracruz, Italy Milan and Italy Catania missions, and was a counselor to the mission president in Buenos Aires and Montevideo, Uruguay. He was a regional representative form 1972-79, and served a mission in Argentina. He also served two stake missions. He was once treasurer for the Church's building committee in South America.

Sister Boren, a medical laboratory technician, is also a native of Argentina and , like her husband, speaks English, Spanish and Italian. She served with her husband in Uruguay, Mexico and Italy and has worked in various auxiliaries. They are parents of four children.

Another very interesting article about Samuel Boren, by Kevin Stoker ,appeared in the section "Missionary Moments" and was titled, "A well-placed pen." (See page?)

Before the dedication of the temple, the advance man was preparing the mission vehicle (Toyota Land Cruiser) to chauffeur President Hinckley in. President Christensen mentioned that the missionaries were probably the most active members of the Church in Peru and yet they had no invitation to attend the temple, and they had been instructed on a number of occasions that they couldn't attend without First Presidency invitation or approval. It was also mentioned that it would be very special if he and other General Authorities might meet with the missionaries in both the North as well as the South Missions to have a special meeting for a short time just to inspire them in the missionary efforts.

The brother, acting as President Hinkley's security guard and driver, indicated to President Christensen that it was not his place to arrange those things, but if he felt impressed at the right moment to maybe mention that they had not received that invitation. Nothing was heard back until one of the sessions President Hinckley noticed that the missionaries weren't in attendance and wanted to extend a special invitation to them. He also requested that he have a special meeting with them on Sunday night after the dedication services were over before he flew out. The prayers of the missionaries were answered and those missionaries working in Lima had the opportunity to sit at the feet of six General Authorities, one member of the First Presidency, an Apostle, and four members of the First Quorum of the Seventy and hear their counsel and inspiration to further the work here in Peru. This was great inspiration to all missionaries who attended.

One example of President Hinkley's love and concern for each missionary is expressed in a thoughtful letter received by President Christensen, dated February 5, 1986, from President Gordon B. Hinckley. He wrote:

> Thank you for your handwritten note of January 1986 expressing appreciation on behalf of your missionaries to attend the Lima, Peru Temple dedication and also the missionary meeting which we held Sunday evening.
>
> My only regret is that all of the missionaries in that area were not advised earlier. Most of them really will never have an opportunity to attend a temple dedication, and I am very glad that things worked out as they did, even though the notice was short.
>
> It was a pleasure to see you and Sister Christensen. I am confident that you are having a wonderful time, and I know that you are doing great good. Our prayers are with you.

Brother Paul Lindeman wrote, "It was a very spiritual experience to be in the Peru Temple when President Gordon B. Hinkley gave the dedicatory prayer. I was Recorder of the Temple and trained some of the native people who were hired to work in the Recorders office. Record keeping is a very sacred part of the Lord's Church as you know."

Chapter 14

The Stone Rolls Forth

In the March 14, 1987 edition of the "Church News" the following article mentioned the missionary work in Peru:

> More missionaries are now serving than ever before in the history of the Church . . . Coupled with . . . the most extensive missionary circulation ever of the Book of Mormon. Numerous missionaries have told of the Book's conversion power. The 1986 total for placement was 2,911,916. Of these, 15 percent, or 447,598, included personal photos and testimonies provided through the Family-to-Family Book of Mormon program.
>
> Many of the books were placed in Central and South American countries. The Book of Mormon's influence is dramatically illustrated in a recent account from the Peru Lima South Mission: Elder Michael K. Taylor of Lakeland, Florida, and his companion, Elder Jovino Sedano, Huacho, Peru, met with a woman they described as an evangelist and the leader of a large evangelical congregation. The Elders didn't know at the time, but she'd had a strong impression of a special book years before. She felt another book should accompany the Bible. She'd searched for it -- buying up books from other religions in the quest, but never finding the right one.
>
> As they began the discussion, Elder Taylor brought out a copy of the Book of Mormon and set it on his lap. "That's it! That's the book!" she cried. "I know that book is true." She and five members of her congregation were baptized a short time later.
>
> While other conversions in Peru may not be as dramatic, they are as powerful. The Book of Mormon figures in many conversions, said Mission President Dale Christensen. "We invite the missionaries to share the Book of Mormon with everyone," he said. In that spirit, he and wife, Mary-Jo, helped introduce a tailor

and his family to the Church. The tailor, called in to alter President Christensen's suits, stopped to chat after his work was done. He was given a copy of the Book of Mormon.

The tailor, Jose Quintana, later told the Christensens he'd only accepted the book out of courtesy. But after reading a few pages, he stopped reading it out of courtesy and began reading it as Scripture. He and his family were baptized shortly afterwards by President Christensen. Quintana's first calling to the Church was to serve in a bishopric.

Brother Jose Quintana was a tailor by profession. He served as first counselor in the Rimac Ward Bishopric. He sold his sewing machine and refrigerator to come to the U.S. and visit General Conference in Salt Lake City, Utah. This was a great sacrifice for the whole family.

For one of the final discussions, Brother Quintana and his daughter walked clear across Lima because they didn't have enough money to pay the bus fare for the whole family. When asked why they had done it, he said, "If Brigham Young and the pioneers could walk across the United States for the Gospel, then we can walk across Lima to the mission home to receive our discussion." During his visit to General Conference he shared the following experience upon meeting Apostle David B. Haight at the Peru Lima North Mission home:

As we were walking toward the mission office to pay our money for the support of our son on his mission, President Durrant invited us to come over to the mission car to meet Apostle David B. Haight, as he was just leaving. I greeted him and shook his hand. Then he greeted my wife and took her hand in his. President Durrant was translating and said something in English. Then Elder Haight, still holding my Juana's hand, closed his eyes for several moments as if he were praying. It was as though he knew of my wife's pain and discomfort in her right arm. For weeks she had taken medication and soaked it with almost no relief. As Elder Haight let go of her hand, she was healed and the pain was gone. Everyone said good-bye and the car drove away. She hasn't taken medication or felt any discomfort since that moment. I know he is a true apostle of Jesus Christ."

On January 30-31, 1988 Elder M. Russell Ballard of the Quoram of the Twelve Apostles and Elder Carl Pratt, a Regional Representative and newly called Mission President, came to Lima to create seven new stakes. Lima became the city with the second largest number of stakes of any metropolitan area outside the United States.

Elder Ballard's message was divinely inspired and focused on some of the most powerful and significant aspects dealing with the fulfillment of prophesy and the promises of the Lord as outlined in the Book of Mormon (1 Ne 22:6-9; 2 Ne Ch's 7-8 and 12-24; 3 Ne 16:4-15 and 20; 3 Ne 20:10 - 23:4 and Ether 13:2-13).

He described the destiny of the Lamanite people. Many felt the spirit witness again that he and Elder Carl Pratt as translator, both descendants of the first missionaries to South America, were participating in the fulfillment of the Savior's words in 3 Ne 21:7 in that they now have a "sign" to know that the "covenant" is being and will be fulfilled as promised in 3 Ne 20:25 which says, "Ye are the children of the prophets . . . and in thy seed shall all the kindreds of the earth be blessed." The people of Peru will be a powerful force in preaching the Gospel to all the world, and with the Gentiles, they will help build the New Jerusalem in preparation of Christ's Millennial reign. (Ether 13:6-8)

There were, no doubt, a number of personages on the other side of the veil along with the grandfathers of both Elder Ballard and Elder Pratt who were praising their remarks and sustaining their efforts. This truly was a moment in history!

Sacrifice brings forth the blessings of heaven. On Wednesday, August 22, 1990, while laboring in Huancayo,

Elders Christian Ugarte and Manuel Hidalgo were killed by guerillas from the Shining Path terrorist group. Elder Ugarte lacked about two weeks to finish his mission, and Elder Hidalgo had been out about four months. Elder Ugarte had worked earlier in this city, but had been transferred out after a short stay in Lima. Elder Ugarte requested that he and his then companion Elder Hidalgo, be transferred together back to Huancayo. This transfer was among the last given in June by President Douglas Earl as he completed his mission. It was not a usual thing to transfer a companionship together, and it was even rarer to have a missionary ask for and receive a choice of working areas.

Some time later, as they walked together, they were gunned down and killed by their terrorist assassins. The details of the killing are not so important. But when the missionaries room and belongings were reviewed by mission authorities, it was discovered that the Elders were aware that they were under surveillance. Among the writings of Elder Hidalgo was a repeated reference to his favorite scriptures, D&C 101:32-38 with special emphasis on 35 and 36:

> 35. And all they who suffer persecution for my name and endure in faith, though they are called to lay down their lives for my sake, yet shall they partake of all this glory.
> 36. Wherefore, fear not even unto death; for in this world your joy is full, but in me your joy is full.

He had shared that belief in his last interview with his mission President. When the Area Presidency contacted the family of Elder Ugarte, who had been born a member of the church to one of the first families in Trujillo, his mother said that he had come to her in a dream a couple of nights before and had told her that he would die.

The family of Elder Hidalgo, who had not been members very long, did not react the same way. Regardless of what Elder Hartman Rector did or said, they were very upset and he was not sure whether he would even be welcome at the funeral. The morning of the funeral, the mother welcomed him and the funeral went off fine. Later, she revealed that her son, had come to her in the night and told her things that calmed her. Elder Rector told her that the family could be sealed together in the temple if they would get ready. In January of 1991, the Hidalgo family were sealed together. Elder Dana Nottinghim, Elder Hidalgo's first companion was the proxy for his fallen companion.

There were threats and attacks on others lives and on several chapels. Shortly thereafter, all north Americans were taken out of the country for security reasons. The Peruvian leadership, missionaries and members continued faithfully and with great success to build up the Kingdom over the following years. Because of their faithfulness in keeping the commandments, peace came once again to this great country. Special fasting and prayers for the church and government leaders have brought forth the blessings from heaven. They began to prosper and the doors were opened again to having foreign missionaries to enter the country.

It has been reported that the work is going forward better than ever and the members are waiting with great anticipation for another and then another temple to be constructed in Peru. Such is the Lord's work as it moves forward to bless the lives of all who would hear and accept this glad message. This history will continue and be added up as the days and years progress. Each member, each missionary, each church leader and prophet is a part of The History of the Church in Peru. This history is true and is another testimony of our Lord and Savior Lord Jesus Christ. Amen.

Made in the USA
Las Vegas, NV
04 March 2021